ADVANCE PRAISE

"*The best leaders do not leave their humanity at the office door and Sally-Anne understands this better than most people I know. In* Mindful Command *she conveys with supreme clarity that what's important in leadership is not what you do, but who you are and how you do it. Her recipe for developing that magic alignment has been supercharging her clients' impact for years. Now we can all benefit, and no evolving leader should be without this refined and delightfully readable book.*"

BRIAN GARISH

President, Mars Veterinary Health International

"*In her naval career, Sally-Anne embodied the human qualities essential to leadership excellence and was a role model for other women. Now a distinguished leadership coach, her presence and wisdom are an inspiration to people in all walks of life. In this beautifully and concisely written guide, she shares her simple, effective leadership development framework and the powerful tools and practices that make it work. I wholeheartedly recommend this book to anyone aspiring to develop their leadership presence and skill.*"

VICE ADMIRAL SIR DAVID STEEL

Governor and Commander-in-Chief Gibraltar,
Second Sea Lord and Chief of Naval Personnel 2012-2015

"*Sally-Anne has an exceptional understanding of what good leadership is, and the clarity of thought and expression which she brings to her coaching practice is evident on every page of* Mindful Command. *This is a superb distillation of her long experience of what really works, in a brief, outstandingly readable and well-structured form. For busy leaders seeking to master themselves and to improve their impact in any situation, this is a go-to guide to keep handy at all times.*"

FRANCISCO LOBBOSCO

Group CEO, FutureLife

"This is an immensely valuable book for anyone who would like to understand what good leadership behaviours look like and would like to improve their own leadership. It is a concise, pragmatic and very enjoyable 'manual' devoid of management jargon which requires some self-analysis by the reader but which will be very well rewarded."

PAUL (PABLO) ETTINGER

Chairman, TALENTBANQ, One of the founding team, Caffè Nero

"This book reminded me immediately of F. Scott Fitzgerald's famous test of intelligence as the tolerance of paradox: 'the ability to hold two ideas in mind at the same time and still function'. Sally-Anne lives this paradox in Mindful Command. *With simplicity and clarity, she provides a different, more soulful and deeper human reflection on leadership than is usually found in books on this much treated subject. Easy and quick to read,* Mindful Command *offers not only insight and wisdom, but, more importantly, real-world application."*

SQUADRON LEADER JOHN PETERS

Former Gulf War POW, author, business coach

"This is a book that every leader needs in their life – a wonderfully clear and concise reference for busy leaders who want to continuously improve their impact. Sally-Anne's wisdom shines through and her view of leadership as an integral part of life resonates perfectly with the vision of so many purpose-driven entrepreneurs. Her Mindful Command model is a brilliantly simple and effective one to hold in mind, and the book is one you'll want to come back to again and again."

LAURENCE MCCAHILL

Founder, The Happy Startup School

"As Jones and Goffee said, 'powerful leadership is all about being yourself, with skill'. In this accessible gem of a book Sally-Anne gives us a genuinely usable and practical framework to support the vital inner work that sustains effective authentic leadership. Whether you are developing your own leadership, or supporting leadership in others, you have in your hands a key resource."

DIANE NEWELL

Editor of *Coaching and Mentoring*, Managing Director Discovery, The OCM Group

"Sally-Anne is an inspirational coach with a wonderful talent for creating clarity out of confusion. Her book exemplifies that skill. The tools and practices really work, and Sally-Anne's integrated Mindful Command model makes sense of them all. On top of that the book is a great read, packed with fascinating stories. It deserves a wide readership. Highly recommended."

JACK HUBBARD
Founder, Propellernet

"Sally-Anne's incisive and engaging book penetrates right to the heart of the potential we all have to become the leaders, parents, partners and friends we want to be. Leadership is not a role, it's a way of being, and Mindful Command offers a way of embodying that. This is a gift not only to leaders, but to all who aspire to live better, serve others and make the world a better place."

PROFESSOR KEES KLOMP
Professional changemaker, purpose business consultant, mentor, author, speaker and entrepreneur

"Sally-Anne's book captures an important nuance of leadership through storytelling and blends her experience with a wealth of practical guidance. Through her powerful framework, Mindful Command, she reminds us that how we choose to travel on our personal journey makes the essential difference to how we show up and lead."

LARISSA HARRISON
Global HR Director

"This timely, wise and practical book is the perfect companion to help leaders become more present, aware, compassionate and aligned with purpose – all so sorely needed in these times. Be warned – this book may change your life dramatically, and have a marked impact on those around you."

LIZ HALL
Editor of Coaching at Work, leadership coach, mindfulness trainer and author of Mindful Coaching and Coach your Team

Published by
LID Publishing
An imprint of LID Business Media Ltd.
LABS House, 15-19 Bloomsbury Way,
London, WC1A 2TH, UK

info@lidpublishing.com
www.lidpublishing.com

A member of:

BPR ⊛

businesspublishersroundtable.com

Printed and bound in Great Britain by Halstan Ltd
ISBN: 978-1-911687-46-7
ISBN: 978-1-911687-47-4 (ebook)

Cover and page design: Caroline Li

SALLY-ANNE AIREY

MINDFUL COMMAND

THE WAY OF THE EVOLVING LEADER

MADRID | MEXICO CITY | LONDON
BUENOS AIRES | BOGOTA | SHANGHAI

DEDICATION

TO MY SONS, HUGO AND ELLIOT,
WITH ALL MY LOVE.

CONTENTS

INTRODUCTION

STARTING OUT

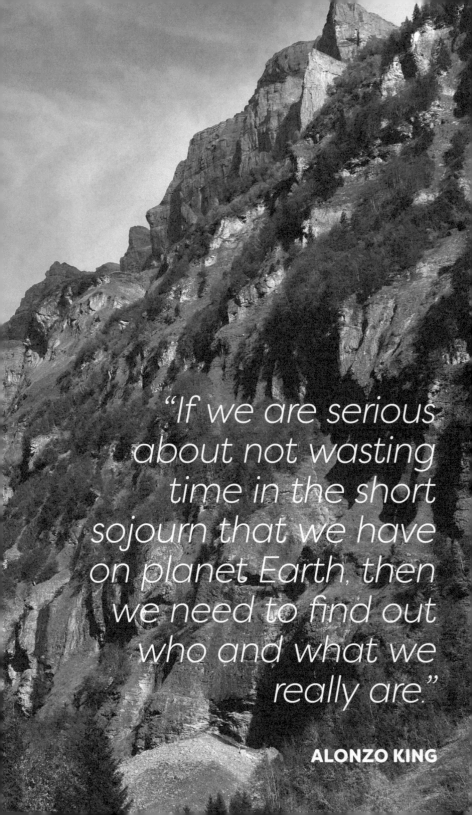

"If we are serious about not wasting time in the short sojourn that we have on planet Earth, then we need to find out who and what we really are."

ALONZO KING

What does it mean to be a truly good leader?

My own experience has led me to the conclusion that leadership starts with who we are and how we impact others; it's about engaging people to get the right things done, in such a way that everyone flourishes.

In all the leaders I've known, what distinguishes the good from the great is the capacity to quieten all the voices in their head and speak only from their own true voice. They are at one with themselves. When they speak, people listen.

Those leaders have certain qualities in common: they are aware, clear, grounded, stable, and not afraid to speak and act for what is right. These are qualities which every one of us can evolve within ourselves.

––––––––––––––

Our capacity to be a good leader grows as we grow; and gets stuck as we get stuck. The way is long and winding, with many twists and turns.

People have been leading one another for as long as they have been walking the earth, and countless people have shared theories, models, tools and advice about how to lead well. Now, based on my own experience, I'm distilling this guide to what really matters in leadership, why it works and how you can develop more of it for yourself.

The central thread is a leadership framework – Mindful Command – that I've developed over some years of teaching our Evolving Leadership programme. It has been tried, tested and refined several times over. The many leaders whose lives Mindful Command has changed are the ones urging me to share it with you here.

———————

This book is intentionally concise.

In the first chapter I clarify the origin of Mindful Command and what I mean by it. In the second and third I explore the characteristics of skilful leadership and ways of working on yourself to navigate all the things that get in the way.

Chapters four to seven explore and illustrate the four foundations of Mindful Command. Each of these can stand alone, but together they are stronger and more complete; and each one contains elements of the other three.

I hope you find something here for you. Finding your way to skilful leadership is not a linear process. Go where your attention takes you. Dip in and out. Play with the tools and practices you consider most helpful to where you are now. See what resonates with you.

I want to inspire and encourage you to become the leader you can be. That leader is evolving within you, right now.

A WORD ABOUT ME

In 1981, after university, I joined the Royal Navy to become an officer, at a time when women did not have the right to serve at sea nor even to continue serving once they were pregnant. Courageous, fair leadership was part of the Navy's DNA, but equality of opportunity for men and women, for which I advocated vigorously, came only ten years later. When I left the Navy in 2004, I was a Commander and the Navy's first serving mother.

Over those 23 years, as well as leading teams of my own in diverse management roles, I worked with many leaders – some great, some not-so-great. I realized the key difference between them was not so much *what* they did, but *how* they did it, and how they motivated their people to give of their best.

After the Navy, I lived and worked for eight years in Ukraine and Russia, as business manager of a rapidly expanding international school in Kyiv, and then, by chance, as a leadership coach. I was asked to help a French manager in a German company and discovered a talent that became my vocation. I also encountered mindfulness for the first time; my daily practice, now in its 15th year, sits at the heart of my coaching approach. After professional qualification as a coach with The OCM in Oxford, I worked with leaders in multinational companies in Kyiv, Moscow and across Europe.

Since 2013 my principal focus has been my own leadership development business, based in the French Alps near Geneva.

CHAPTER ONE

WHAT IS MINDFUL COMMAND?

"Mind is the master weaver."

JAMES ALLEN

Good leadership is an inside out affair.

People who lead others well usually lead themselves well. People who do not lead themselves well rarely lead others well.

As I write this now, it seems obvious. Reading it now, you may well be thinking the same. And yet, very few of the leaders I've worked with have ever really given it this much thought. Those who have, and want to explore it more, rarely know where to start.

In response to this, I devoted a year to devising a nine-month, part-time leadership programme for a group of eight different leaders who had the same enquiry:

> Who am I?
> How do I relate to the world?
> How do I want to evolve as a leader?

I called it Evolving Leadership and launched it in 2019. At the time of writing, the programme is in its fifth year and has itself evolved – to the point at which I feel ready to share its principles more widely.

Each year, the new participants in the Evolving Leadership programme meet online for the first time in March. They come together in person twice in the mountains of the French Alps where I live, and part in November as trusted friends. What each of them carries forward is the in-between: everything that has happened in the relational space between us all. At first, this can be difficult to put into words. It's usually unlike anything they've known before.

The basis of their learning experience is a leadership framework which I call Mindful Command. This unusual juxtaposition of apparently contradictory ideas – mindful and command – stems from my own experience of leadership and mindfulness and arose from a conversation with my friend and collaborator, Charles Davies, originator of Very Clear Ideas,[1] who was smart enough to suggest it to me.

The command in Mindful Command speaks to what I learned about leadership in my naval career. Naval leadership is centred on the military concepts of 'commander's intent' and 'mission command.' Commander's intent is a leader's clear statement of the desired outcome of an operation, including its purpose, objectives and the resources required. This can be at any level. Mission command combines the commander's intent with delegated freedom of action, initiative, responsiveness and flexibility. The *why* and the *what* are clarified up front, and the people responsible for its execution are empowered to decide on the *how*.

The mindful in Mindful Command comes from my own mindfulness practice and relates to a leader's level of awareness, presence and impact. More on that later.

There's nothing military or directive about Mindful Command. Separately, mission command and mindfulness stand alone. Together, they help you cultivate the capacity to show up, whatever the circumstance, as your clear, calm, centred self, confident of doing the right thing.

Ultimately, Mindful Command is a holistic foundation for clear, courageous, compassionate leadership – represented simply here:

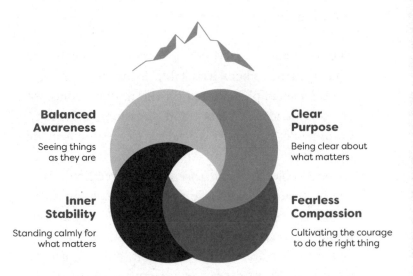

Balanced Awareness
Seeing things as they are

Clear Purpose
Being clear about what matters

Inner Stability
Standing calmly for what matters

Fearless Compassion
Cultivating the courage to do the right thing

Balanced awareness amplifies clear purpose; clear purpose fuels fearless compassion; fearless compassion channels balanced awareness and clear purpose into action; inner stability enables them all to evolve.

Held by the mountain, and with space at its core, Mindful Command offers you a way of showing up – i.e. being present – which is natural to you and generates positive impact.

This means being at one with yourself and is like having an inner space you call your 'safe haven,' akin to a state of inner peace. You see things as they are. You're clear about what matters. You hold your ground, you speak truth and you have the courage to do what is right.

Some leaders may seem to be naturally at one with themselves. If we think of some generally recognized great leaders, such as Nelson Mandela, Mahatma Gandhi or Mother Teresa, this may well be the image we have of them. But I doubt they always are (or were). Every one of them is human, just like us. They have their struggles too.

At one with yourself is possibly one of the toughest things to be. We all carry our own burdens, and society does little to lighten the load.

———————

One leader I worked with recently found this especially difficult. As a relatively young leader in a global organization, David had worked tirelessly to fast-track his career to the senior position he now occupied. But instead of feeling good about his achievement, he was anxious, agitated and full of self-doubt.

"Things are moving too slowly," he told me.

I asked him what "too slowly" meant to him. He told me about the job he wanted next and his frustration that it was taking too long to get there. He felt he was ready for this promotion, whereas others – including his line manager – didn't agree.

I asked him what he enjoyed about where he was now. He looked surprised.

"Enjoy?" he said. "I don't think I enjoy anything. Except perhaps my family. But I'm not even sure I'm any good at that."

David was questioning the point of it all. He felt lost. He'd done the things he thought were important to success in life. But none of his successes was ever good enough. He always felt he had more to prove.

In our work together over the months that followed, I helped David see things as they were (rather than as he told himself they were) and focus on what mattered the most. As he became more present as a leader, partner and parent, his perspective slowly shifted.

"I was overly worried about the future," he told me later. "I had unrealistic expectations of myself. Career-wise I'm not worried anymore. Now I'm just focusing on being the best version of me. I have shaky moments, but they're short-lived. Mainly, I'm massively enjoying the here and now. I don't over-prepare for things like I used to. I feel genuinely curious. I'm spending more time with my family and friends. My work is better for it."

Massively enjoying the here and now. Being kinder to himself. Staying curious. Focusing on being his best. It was as if a weight had been lifted from David's shoulders. To his line manager and others, it was a "spectacular shift." To his family, they had their husband and father back.

So, how did that happen? There may have been a few 'lightbulb moments,' but mainly things moved forward for David incrementally, over time. Together we explored how he could be more patient with himself, and value the things that brought him joy over things that did not. What he previously mistrusted, he began to accept. He got clear on what he could control and what he had to let go. He got better at seeing things as they are. As he became more open, he trusted himself more and lost his fear of speaking his truth.

All the little shifts added up to one big one: a sense of freedom. "I feel like my old self again," he said. When I asked him if he felt at one with himself, he was able to say yes. Because now he knew what I meant.

With my support and encouragement, David did the inner work necessary to clarify what mattered most and commit to making it happen every day.

He maintained his resolve by staying firmly grounded in the here and now: working with what was possible and doing this again and again until it became his new way.

By repeating these things consistently over time, David gained inner strength and renewed self-belief. He showed up in the way he'd really wanted to all along.

If you are prepared to do this inner work for yourself, the Mindful Command framework offers you a place to start. Its foundations, and the tools and practices within them, provide tangible support along your way. Balancing your awareness, clarifying your purpose, stabilizing your centre and acting compassionately are all things you can learn to do. When you integrate them into your way of being, they become the stable ground on which skilful leadership can evolve.

Acting with Mindful Command builds a combination of skills that support your capacity to create space for yourself and hold space for others. To hold space is to sit with someone and listen non-judgmentally to what they are trying to express, without trying to fix it for them or influence the outcome.

To give you a baseline understanding of how you currently relate to the Mindful Command framework,

I encourage you to complete the following simple assessment. Then, when you've finished reading and digesting the principles, tools and practices in this book, I suggest you do the assessment again and note what has changed.

"So many things
I would have done,
but clouds got
in my way."

JONI MITCHELL

MINDFUL COMMAND
SELF-ASSESSMENT

Foundations of Mindful Command
Balanced Awareness **– seeing things as they are** **In any situation I am able to:**
1. Observe my own thoughts.
2. Identify my own feelings.
3. Focus on the person/people with whom I am speaking.
4. Ask questions and listen fully to understand the full context of the situation.
5. I fully commit, mind and body aligned, to the decision.
6. Be present and ask myself, "What is needed right now?"
Clear Purpose **– being clear about what matters**
7. I am clear on my life purpose.
8. I am clear about what matters most to me.
9. I connect my purpose to my work.
10. I am clear about how I make my decisions.

Rate yourself on each behavioural scale:
Never, **R**arely, **S**ometimes, **F**requently, **A**lways.

	N	R	S	F	A

Foundations of Mindful Command

Fearless Compassion **– cultivating the courage to do the right thing**
11. I identify and acknowledge what I am feeling in any moment.
12. I accept my feelings without judgment.
13. I acknowledge others' feelings.
14. I listen to others and accept them without judgment.
15. I act courageously in service of what I know is right.
Inner Stability **– standing calmly for what matters**
16. I slow down to listen to my body.
17. I know when I am not centred and calm.
18. I quieten my thoughts and feelings at will.
19. I am resilient in the face of a challenge.
20. I move my body as a form of connection to myself.
Holding Space **– being physically, mentally and emotionally present**
21. In moments of tension I pause, notice what is triggering me and create space to respond consciously.
22. I do not judge myself while I am working through an issue.
23. I am patient with others while they work through their own challenges.
24. I do not judge others while they are sharing their journey.
25. I do not try to step in and 'fix' others.

	N	R	S	F	A

CHAPTER TWO

FIVE SIGNS OF SKILFUL LEADERSHIP

"If you get the
inside right,
the outside will
fall into place."

ECKHART TOLLE

Skilful leadership is knowing who you are, understanding your impact and leading others to get the right things done in the right way.

A leadership journey is personal, and universal. Your experience is our experience. There is nothing you are going through that we, human beings everywhere, have not gone through. There is much we can learn from one other.

The way of the evolving leader stretches through your entire life. The signs along the way help you steer your course.

These are the signs that will keep you on track.

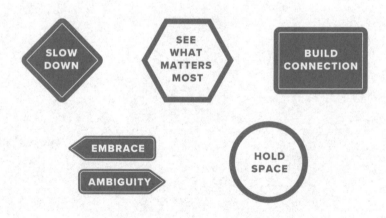

SLOW DOWN

There was once someone who was capable, yet uncertain; energetic, yet lacking self-confidence; decisive, yet unnecessarily apologetic; purposeful, yet looking for something.

That someone was me. But I didn't know it.

I didn't know it because I rarely slowed down for long enough to notice.

In those days my fast-paced, quick-thinking capability was applauded by a series of bosses who would reward me for "achieving more in one day than most people do in a week." My successes built my reputation, and my reputation formed my identity. To everyone else, I seemed to be thriving on it.

One day, as I was running – literally – from one office to the next, I heard a senior colleague shout out, "Walk! Running frightens the troops." It stopped me in my tracks. I moved on, more slowly.

I began to realize that I ran, everywhere, all the time. Not just physically, mentally too. My quick thinking had an urgency to it. My actions followed. I didn't know any other way.

There's a time for running and a time for walking. I'd confused the two. I'd allowed the pace of everything outside me to dictate the pace of everything inside me.

Nearly all the leaders I work with feel like I did then: overworked, overwrought and often overwhelmed. Rushing to catch up, but not quite sure what they're rushing to catch up with.

In the words of poet and author David Whyte:

> The great tragedy of speed as an answer
> to the complexities and responsibilities
> of existence is that very soon we cannot
> recognize anything or anyone who is not
> travelling at the same velocity as we are.

Like sitting on a high-speed train, the landscape whooshing past so fast that it blurs your vision. Move too fast for too long, and you lose sight of what is right before your eyes.

All the leaders I've ever worked with want the opposite of this. They want more time, more space, more calm in their lives. No one ever wants more meaningless speed.

Every one of them, like you, wants to lead well. Every leader, like you, also wants to parent well and be a good partner and friend. None of this is possible if you don't stop to notice. When you do, when you simply pause and look, and listen, something changes.

Pause for a moment now.
Tune into your breathing.

Look around you. What do you see?
Whatever it is, look at it as if for the first time.

What do you notice?

What you notice doesn't matter right now. What matters is that you notice it. In doing so, you're developing your capacity to be present and aware.

Learning how to slow down gave me time and space to listen. I became less distracted, more present. And I began to realize that however fast I ran, I would never get there. Because there is no there. There is only here.

I know I'm not alone in this. Many of the highly accomplished people I encounter spend much of their time chasing something *out there* at the expense of what matters *right here*. It is, perhaps, the greatest irony of the world we've created that it makes the most natural thing of all – simply being here – the most difficult.

If leaders like us want to make an impact in the world, we must understand how to be here, in the present. Because it's only in the present that impact is made. Impact is meant to be felt. If we're not present, fully 'showing up,' it can't be felt.

We have created this high-speed world for better or worse. There is much beyond our control. But there is plenty within our control too. When you slow yourself down, you slow time down. You create the space, to quote Tibetan-Buddhist teacher and writer, Pema Chödrön, for, "the very scary step of getting to know yourself."

Slowing down and getting to know yourself are key to evolving skilfully as a leader.

"Between he who has conquered a hundred thousand men in battle and he who has conquered himself, it is the latter who is the greatest victor."

MASTER OK-SUNG-ANN-BARON

SEE WHAT MATTERS MOST

I owe everything I know about leadership to all the leaders I've worked with – good and bad, in the Navy and beyond – and to the teams and individuals I've led myself. Among them are a few whose impact spread far and wide, and from whom I learned so much. From my time in the Navy, there's one who stands out.

In 1989, Admiral Sandy Woodward was appointed Commander-in-Chief of the Navy's Home Command. I was his Flag Lieutenant, or personal aide.

I remember how thrilled I was to be working directly for the former task force commander of the Falklands War, and equally how apprehensive. I needn't have worried. From the very first moment, he was just himself.

He also saw something in me that I'd not yet seen, and he encouraged me to submit an article arguing for equal opportunity to a distinguished naval journal. It was published and I was later told it helped inform the subsequent work on gender equality in the Armed Forces. In 1991, women were finally allowed to assume front line military roles. For the Navy, that meant women could at last serve in warships at sea.

What stood out for me in Sandy Woodward were not his military successes, nor his razor-sharp intellect. More important than those, in my view, was his genuine humanity. He could be demanding, impatient, brusque, and he was not universally popular, but he had an unerring ability to get to the heart of what mattered, and act on it. And he was kind, not nice. You knew where you stood with him.

He once told me about a difficult choice he faced soon after taking command of the nuclear-powered submarine HMS *Warspite* in 1969. One year earlier, the vessel had been involved in a Cold War underwater collision with a Soviet submarine in the Barents Sea.[2] *Warspite* had been knocked over under water to an angle of almost 75 degrees, had swung back like a pendulum, hit the other vessel a second time and been knocked over again.

Many of the crew were badly shaken and in the control room, one sailor was so gripped by panic that he refused to release the steering mechanism and had to be forcibly removed. Quick reactions by others enabled the submarine to emergency-surface, as did the Soviet vessel. There were no serious casualties in either. *Warspite* had incurred significant damage but was able to dive again and limp home to the UK. The public story was that she had collided with an iceberg and the crew was required to keep the true circumstances secret.

One year on, the submarine was newly repaired but not yet tested. Many of the crew were still shaken by the incident and had lost confidence in the boat's capability and safety.[3] They were nervously anticipating what their new Commanding Officer would be like.

Calmly and without fuss, Woodward took the submarine and its crew out on a training exercise in which he included a series of extreme underwater manoeuvres, emergency dives and surfacings. These culminated in a very steep and rapid dive which took the submarine to the limit of its safe diving depth before pulling out.

In doing this, he was clear that what mattered most was gaining the complete confidence of his crew. He judged that nothing less than a comprehensive demonstration of the submarine's capability would enable this. He understood the risks and he had the necessary technical knowledge and skills to minimize them. He also understood what his people were capable of, even if they themselves doubted it. He was prepared to take them to the edge of fear, confident he could bring them back. He made a difficult choice, for the right reasons. This was a calculated risk, but not a gamble. In leadership this is a critical distinction. Woodward saw what mattered most and had the courage to do what was necessary to achieve it.

His crew realized this. He won their trust and their respect.

———————

Thirteen years later, when the Falklands War was about to break, Admiral Woodward was in the right place at the right time to take command of the naval and air forces. Their role was to land and support the soldiers and Royal Marines on the ground. Woodward's role, above all else, was to make the tough decisions, often with incomplete information, on which people's lives depended.

In his memoirs of that period, *One Hundred Days: The Memoirs of the Falklands Battle Group Commander*, he reveals his personal struggle with some of the decisions required of him and their impact on the people around him. "The scene has greatly changed," he wrote in a letter home to his wife, "I am having to alter my ways." He realized that he needed to listen better to what others needed of him.

This reflection speaks to every committed leader in any context – business, politics, education, medical or any other – faced with an impossible task. Impossible, because in the end there is never a real winner or loser. There are gains and losses along the way and neither victory nor defeat is ever complete. The best a leader can do – and this is a great deal – is draw on their full human capacity to adapt and commit to what the context demands of them.

Ultimately, the leader's job is to confront the difficult challenge and make the right decision. They must understand all aspects of the task at hand and properly consider the people involved. The higher the stakes, and the greater the risk, the sharper their focus needs to be on what matters and what action is necessary to achieve it. They must also accept that mistakes will occur and be ready to course correct. In other words, the leader's job is to roll strategy, tactics and the welfare of their people into one.

Having a clear vision of what matters most and the courage to act on it are key to evolving skilfully as a leader.

BUILD
CONNECTION

In September 2022, people from all over the world travelled to London to pay their final respects to Queen Elizabeth II, whose death ended her 70-year reign. In perhaps the biggest show of human solidarity the world had known outside a war zone, tens of thousands of people joined a miles-long queue snaking through the streets of London. They readily faced a wait of more than 24 hours to see the Queen lying in state in Westminster Hall.

The quality of that experience reminds me of a Friday evening over 40 years ago. It was snowing heavily. I and thousands of others were jostling for a seat on one of the few trains leaving London's Paddington station. When I finally managed to embark on the one train heading west, there was very tight standing room only. Happy simply to be on board, no one was allowing the discomfort to bother them. Spirits were high. People shared food and drink, stories, laughter, with complete strangers. We all faced the long journey ahead with gratitude, even as the train stopped at every station on its circuitous route.

There it was: the spirit of human connection, alive and well, just as it was among those people waiting in line to see the person who for them represented something personally important. New friendships formed that could last a lifetime, joined forever by this unique experience.

> A gathering of souls
> Reaching out
> Beyond ill-defined limits
> For what's been here
> All along.

These words from evolutionary ecologist Alan Rayner in his poem, *The People's Dearest*, remind us of what, deep down, we know: for all those who want to divide and conquer, there are many more of us who want to unite and embrace. It's my firm belief that this is our natural state. When we inhabit it openly, we are at our best.

My friends at The Happy Startup School[4] understand this well. For their community of purpose-driven entrepreneurs, founders Laurence McCahill and Carlos Saba create and foster experiences that bring people together in a way few others do. Their annual Summercamp, in the middle of a large field in the UK, reaches the parts of us – the generous, loving parts – we more usually constrain. In just three days you leave feeling more human, and a lot happier for it.

In these and other 'all in the same boat' scenarios, the context is powerful enough to cut through the behaviours of prejudice and intolerance that pull us apart. In natural disasters, for example, studies show that people put differences aside and come together as one to help vulnerable individuals, families and communities. In situations such as these, the universal spirit of human compassion almost always prevails.

What does this mean for us as leaders?

When we remember that within every person is a human being struggling to find their way, we tap into our capacity to see people as they are: flawed human beings, just like us. This way of seeing people engenders compassion. Compassion feeds human connection. Human connection builds relationships.

In our increasingly socially estranged world (at least in many developed western countries), relationship-building matters more than ever. When relationships are strong, anything is possible. Without them, little can get done.

Those of us who have watched Ted Lasso – the fictional American football coach – in action on our screens have seen this playing out before our eyes. While the character may be fictitious, his values mirror those of many other great sports coaches – like the legendary John Wooden or Valorie Kondos Field – who win not by seeking to win, but by seeing their players as people they want to get to know.

The reason why 'the Ted Lasso way' has captured the hearts and minds of so many is, I believe, because so many want more leaders like him: capable of seeing the best in people, so that their best is what they become.

Seeing people as they are and building meaningful connection are key to evolving skilfully as a leader.

EMBRACE
AMBIGUITY

A big question for leaders today (and one I am often asked) is this: "What does healthy leadership look and feel like?" In other words, how can leaders act in a way that balances a healthy responsibility for individual, team and environmental wellbeing with the need to get things done?

What's interesting here is the underlying assumption that these are an 'either–or.' This is not true.

By challenging your own assumptions and paying attention to what matters, you *can* build positive human connection and develop ways of making the difference you want in the way you want.

Take Jane. A senior leader in a multinational corporation, there were tensions in the leadership team she'd recently joined. They were under huge cost pressure and had to identify financial savings. Toxic behaviours – underhand actions, unconstructive comments – were on the rise. Some leaders had publicly voiced negative insinuations about their colleagues' performance, including hers, which had thrown her onto the back foot. She wondered how to respond effectively.

"Is there any truth in their comments?" I asked her. All of them, she said, contained partial truths, taken out of context and intended to undermine.

I asked her what she was afraid of. "My biggest fear," she said, "is that this team becomes a major energy drainer. What annoys me most is that we're wasting our time."

"Wasting our time?" I queried.

After a long pause, she clarified, "Because we're no longer working for the greater good."

Ah.

Her colleagues' behaviours had touched Jane's core values. Honesty, integrity and trust mattered to her. She was feeling all this at a deeply personal level.

I invited her to pause, take a step back and look at the whole context. What was happening? What were the key contributing factors?

Looking at each team member individually, what was going on for them? What did she imagine might be *their* fears?

Gradually she saw they were all struggling. There were big challenges, immense uncertainty and no clear way ahead. Instead of working through it together, some were attempting to seize control in unhealthy ways.

Once Jane saw this, her feelings toward her colleagues shifted from mistrust to compassion, from helpless to helpful – cautiously at first, then gradually more openly. This fortified her resolve to act well.

She decided to take ownership of her own behaviours and to role model those she wanted to see more of in the leadership team: respect, active listening, collaboration, trust. She also committed to setting clear boundaries, stating her needs and holding her ground.

The forthcoming out-of-office team event would be the perfect opportunity to practise, she said, smiling. It was good to see the humour back in her eyes.

Jane may have wished the context were otherwise, but she worked with it as it was. She dug into her own inner resources and focused on what she could control: herself. This empowered her and gave her courage to act in service of what mattered most to her: the greater good of her team and their work.

This is healthy leadership in action. It's not about right and wrong. In any context involving people and systems, there's no one way. The role of the leader is to step back and evaluate all aspects of the situation, however complex and ambiguous, and make the best decision possible in the circumstances. To do this well, they must take a balanced internal and external view of what's needed.[5]

In our increasingly complex and ambiguous world, a reliable measure of healthy leadership is the leader's ability to respond with care and compassion for the people involved, and with a clear understanding of what the context demands.

Working with ambiguity in a caring, compassionate way is key to evolving skilfully as a leader.

HOLD SPACE

Pausing and stepping back gave Jane the space she needed to see the whole picture. She was able to suspend her habitual reactions: to notice them but not let them take control. Instead, she sat with them for a while, tuning into her feelings and watching her thoughts ebb and flow like waves in her mind.

In this way, Jane could observe what was happening with less personal attachment. She became less judgmental, more curious.

"Between stimulus and response," said Viktor Frankl, "there is a space. And in that space lies our freedom and power to choose our responses. In our response lies our growth and freedom."

These words speak to every one of us who has ever jumped in too soon, reacted without thinking, and said or done something we later regret. They also speak to every leader, like you and me, who – through our own insecurity (impatience, frustration, anxiety) – has stolen space from someone else who needed to be heard.

To hold that space for others, we must first know what it feels like to hold it for ourselves.

Pause again for a moment now.
Tune into your breathing.

This time, listen inside. What do you hear?
Whatever it is, do not judge it. Instead,
be curious.

How does this feel to you?

If you're new to the skill of pausing, this may feel strange. With time and patient repetition, it becomes more familiar. The more often you pause, the quicker you grow the inner 'pause muscle' that enables you to stay calm in challenging moments. You pause, breathe and come back to a sense of equilibrium. In this way, you recentre at will. One day you notice you're pausing automatically, and that you feel generally calmer.

As a junior Royal Navy officer under training in the early 1980s, I knew nothing of pausing and holding space. One day I wrote home to ask my father what to do about the very scary prospect of sitting next to a formidable senior officer at an upcoming formal event. In my mind was a vision of three hours of hell.

"You do nothing," my father replied. "But make sure you listen well and ask good questions."

Sure enough, it worked. I listened attentively. At first it was all rather formulaic. After a while, I became genuinely interested in what the person seated next to me was saying. As we got up to leave, he thanked me. I still remember how that felt.

In hindsight, this was my first lesson in holding space. It showed me the value of listening – without judging, or intervening, or trying to share something clever about myself. Instead, putting all of that to one side and simply listening to this apparently formidable person – who, it turned out, was a human being, just like me.

In communication between two or more people, we often swap stories and share experiences. In some circumstances it's just what's needed, and it's fun. But when someone – a colleague, partner, child, friend – approaches you for a conversation, or even just shares something in passing, and you immediately respond with your opinion or with advice on what to do, you may just have missed the point.

Better to pause. Calm your busy mind. Focus on the other person. Hold the space for them to speak. Listen to the precious, unfiltered truth they're trying to express. Let them feel what it's like to be heard with a genuine desire to understand. Offer no unsolicited advice. Stay curious.

In other words: do nothing; simply be there for them.

As writer Albert Camus put it: "Walk beside me... just be my friend."

―――――――

For most of my twin sons' young lives, I was working full time with a lot on my plate. I would often feel too preoccupied to listen properly, or I would put them off. "Not now," I would say, "Mummy is too busy."

Eventually, I realized this was wrong. I resolved, whenever my children needed me, to do my best to pause and listen. In their Christmas card to me that year they wrote, "You've been great this year, Mum. More of the same please."

This is the power of holding space. In doing nothing, you can change everything – for the other person, for you and for your relationship.

Having the capacity to hold space for yourself and others is the cornerstone of skilful evolving leadership.

―――――――

The space at the core of Mindful Command is held by its four interweaving parts.

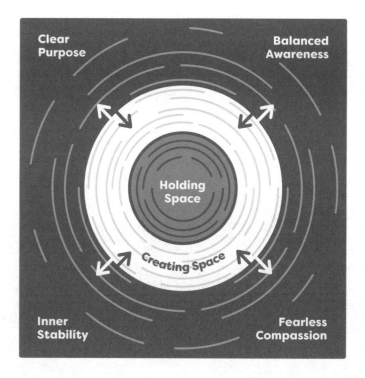

Balancing your awareness, clarifying your purpose, stabilizing your centre and acting compassionately are all things you can learn to do. In doing them you are acting with Mindful Command. You are developing ways of slowing down, seeing what matters most, building connection and embracing ambiguity. This combination of skills builds your capacity to create and hold space for you and the people around you. With practice, they become integral to how you lead.

CHAPTER THREE

PREPARING THE GROUND FOR MINDFUL COMMAND

"*Everyone should know that in the depths of their being lies a realm of silence and peace that is always available, irrespective of the content of their experience.*"

RUPERT SPIRA

The paths surrounding my mountain home are strewn with loose rocks, fallen branches and all kinds of undergrowth. Walk out into nature anywhere and you'll probably encounter something similar.

This is also the way of the evolving leader: occasionally smooth, more often rough. Along the way all kinds of things can cause us to stumble and sometimes fall. They're all part of the journey. Evolving is learning to navigate them with more skill.

———————

It's June 2009. I'm sitting under an oak tree in southwest France. Opposite me is an Italian monk. In 14 simple words, he's just made everything startlingly clear.

"Keep to your practice. When the times comes, you'll know what to do."

I was on my first retreat: one week at the monastic practice centre Village des Pruniers (known more widely as Plum Village), which was founded in 1982 by Zen Master Thich Nhat Hanh. Four days earlier, I'd been listening to this gentle monk teaching us about possibilities for peace. At the end of the talk, something was bothering me, and I asked to speak with him. "Not now," he said. I left, feeling confused.

Meanwhile, the retreat continued. Up at 5am, bed by 10pm. Periods of sitting and walking meditation during the day, different types of community work and more wise teaching.

The day before I was due to leave, the same monk approached me for the first time since our brief exchange. "Would you like to ask your question now?" He suggested we go and sit beneath the tree.

There, in that peaceful spot, looking out over acres of rolling fields, I noticed that the question had lost its power. I asked it anyway. "Look," I said. "I subscribe to peace. But what if there were a circumstance in which protecting my family meant taking lethal action against someone else. What's the right thing to do then?"

"Do you want to harm someone now?" he asked.

"No, not now, but what if...?"

And that's when he spoke the 14 words that changed my life for ever more.

"Keep to your practice. When the times comes, you'll know what to do."

In that week at Plum Village, I touched the joy of simply being present. I was clear, calm and free of judgment. This was distinctly different to my usual way, where my thoughts and feelings would routinely take me forward into the future or back to the past: scenario planning things that may never happen, replaying things that already had or struggling to accept what was happening now. A push and pull that kept me on constant alert.

I liked my new feeling of clarity and calm. I vowed to keep it.

This is where my work – the work I do today – began. It evolved into Mindful Command. Along the way I gained a deeper understanding of what made the work possible: paying attention to the things that get in the way and working with them, not against them.

ACKNOWLEDGING THE REACTIVE SELF

The everyday details of our experience, including the things we repeatedly think, say and do, form the threads of the life we weave for ourselves. To be the leader, parent, partner, friend we want to be, we need to give them our attention.

Pause for a moment.
Tune into your breathing.

Call to mind your usual day.

What do you find yourself repeatedly thinking, saying and doing?

Be curious about this.

Every experience, thought, feeling and physical sensation fires neurons in our brain. The neurons connect and form a pathway. Repetition strengthens the pathway. Non-repetition weakens it.

If the things we find ourselves repeatedly thinking, saying and doing are not aligned with our sense of who we are, we can change them. New neural pathways will form. The brain's structure will adapt. We owe this to the neuroplasticity of the brain, which makes it possible for the brain to change its structure throughout our life.

Simple, but not easy. An ancient almond-shaped structure in our brain called the amygdala can make this very difficult. Located in the midbrain and one of the four main parts of the limbic system, its main function is to regulate emotions such as fear and aggression. Originally it enabled us to react swiftly to fear or threat and in acute circumstances it still does. But when a chronic fear or threat is evoked repeatedly, an overreactive pattern can form in our brain that hijacks rational thinking. We become easily triggered. In certain interactions, before we know it, we've snapped, or recoiled, or frozen, or appeased. This mirrors the brain's acute 'flight, fight, freeze, fawn' stress response.

Afterwards we wonder what we were thinking, and we may realize we weren't thinking at all. The rational thinking part of our brain (the pre-frontal cortex – which evolved long after the limbic system) almost certainly played no part in what happened. What often follows is some form of regret. Until it happens again.

This is the cycle of the reactive self. We all have one. Its many forms are shaped and coloured by our personal experience. But it doesn't define us. It's a part of us that we can change.

———————

Sitting under the tree that day with the Italian monk, my epiphany felt real. To say it changed my life for evermore doesn't mean that from that moment everything was magically OK. It means in that moment I realized that the way through all the noise in my head was to create more moments of peace.

Peace resides in the space we create to be OK with ourselves.

LEARNING
TO PAUSE

Imagine for a moment you're driving a car along a smooth, straight road. The speed limit is 80kph, there's a steady stream of oncoming traffic but ahead of you the road is clear. You're enjoying the drive. Then a car pulls out from a side road in front of you, causing you to brake. The other driver settles into a speed of about 20kph below the limit, for no apparent reason.

If, like me, you find this annoying (and you may not), what typically happens next is something like this: you have an urgent desire to overtake this vehicle. The smart way would be to pull back and position yourself for when a gap appears in the oncoming traffic. But you're aggravated, so instead you get up very close to the vehicle in front and block your view entirely. This antagonizes the other driver, increases your frustration and keeps you stuck where you are.

Your reactive self is getting the better of you. In this and any other everyday situation that triggers you, it's not going to get you to where you want to be.

Welcome to the pause tool. A simple three-step mechanism for creating just enough space to bring the thinking part of your mind back into play.

Step One: Press an imaginary pause button somewhere in your body. If you can, aim for the area around the base of your sternum called the solar plexus.

Step Two: As best you can, bring your attention to that area. Place your hand there; or anywhere else – perhaps your thigh, knee, belly – that supports a sense of connection.

Step Three: Tune into your breathing. Breathe consciously in and out. Observe your breath slowing and deepening. Notice its movement in and out of your body.

There are many ways to ground yourself and you may already have your own way. What matters is that you pause, because pausing gives you space to notice the emotional sensations in your body: tightness in your chest, stomach, throat; clenching of your jaw, shoulders, hands; flushed cheeks. Allow the tension to release: move your body, shake it out; cry if you need to.

When driving a vehicle, you can't fully do the three steps above, but you can at least pause for long enough for your breath to settle. This helps disempower your reactive self. It generates the clearer, calmer state you need to choose how you respond.

Still in the driver's seat but feeling more present, you can see that the way forward is to slow down, pull back, broaden your view, and look for the right moment to move. You see a gap in the oncoming traffic, and you pull out. As you pass the vehicle in front, you notice that what had previously triggered you has lost its power – maybe not fully, but you're at least calmer than you were.

Triggers come in many forms. They provoke your reactive self and put your brain on red alert. Your breath quickens, your heart rate increases and blood is diverted to your major muscle groups to prepare your body to react quickly. All this happens within milliseconds. It once served to keep us all safe and there may be times when you still need it to. But in this reactive state the rational part of your brain gets closed off. You see the world from a reduced perspective.

In most modern-day scenarios, what you need is on the other side of this.

The act of pausing and focusing on your solar plexus diverts attention away from your over-reactive mind and stimulates feelings of inner confidence and control. Breathing in and out and consciously lengthening your outbreath activates sensory receptors in your lungs and throat, which signal to your vagus nerve that you're OK. Your parasympathetic nervous system is engaged, your breath and heart rate slow down.

All of this – which may take minutes rather than seconds – serves to calm and regulate your autonomic nervous system and switch on your rational brain. Your thinking shifts, you see more diverse perspectives, you become more creative.

"When we pause, allow a gap, and breathe deeply," says Tibetan-Buddhist teacher and writer Pema Chödrön, "we can experience instant refreshment. Suddenly we slow down, look out, and there's the world."

To be the leader, parent, partner, friend you want to be, it makes sense to get to know your triggers and use the pause tool to help you respond in the way you really mean to.[6]

"The longest journey you will ever take is the 18 inches from your head to your heart."

THICH NHAT HANH

LEARNING TO LISTEN INSIDE

When you pause, you create a little space to reconnect with yourself and listen inside for what matters. The insight may be momentary, but its effect can turn things around.

The clarity you gain may encourage you to take longer pauses from time to time. It has for me. My pause practice has evolved into longer stretches of sitting or walking in silence to slow down the pace of my life and deepen my insight. By experimenting with what works for me, I've learned to meditate.

Meditation has many forms. All of them are about cultivating something within you. Patient understanding, perhaps; or stillness; or compassion; or courage. Or simply noticing what's arising within you – your thoughts, feelings, sensations, as they are.

Common to each one is your intention, attention and attitude. These inform the conditions for the meditation to unfold. You set your intention, focus your attention and become aware of your body and breath. Scanning from your feet to your crown, settling, and allowing your breath to flow freely.

The form of meditation I mainly practise is known as mindfulness meditation. It has become for me a mainstay in my life and work. These days I cannot imagine either without it.

What I and many others love about mindfulness meditation is the rare opportunity to have no specific expectations and no goal. You're not looking for anything and there's nothing for you to attain. There's no clear beginning and no definitive end. There's no right or wrong, no success and no failure. There's just what's arising within you in any given moment. Mindfulness meditation invites you to be open to noticing it, noticing your reaction to it and letting them both pass.

In the words of renowned meditation teacher Sharon Salzberg:

> You can't fail at mindfulness meditation because what arises is not what's significant. It's how you relate to it. So you can't have the wrong experience. We all want to say: *It was amazing. I had a few seconds of restlessness in the beginning and then this peace, this unfathomable peace just descended upon me, and then began to shimmer at the edges and turn into bliss.* We don't really want to say: *First I was angry, then I was bored, then I got sleepy, then my knee hurt.* But from the point of view of mindfulness,

> it's not a bad sign at all that those things
> happened. It's not even a good sign that the
> other things happened. Everything depends
> on how we relate to them.

This takes practice. We're not used to noticing or feeling things without judging them or ourselves in some way. We're more likely to hold onto them and generally make them into something more than they are. We have physical pain, and we worry about how long it will last. We're disappointed, and we reproach ourselves for not dealing better with the cause of it. When something good happens, we tell ourselves we don't deserve it.

We're not accustomed to noticing or feeling things without some form of bias.

These are all judgments that make our personal experience harder to bear. Accurate judgment is a valuable skill. But when our judgment is unreasonably negative, it can distort our understanding of things.

Mindfulness meditation develops our capacity to see things as they are. We notice the feeling, we notice our reactive judgment, we come back to the feeling and listen to it again. Or we notice we've become caught up in a thought and drifted off, and we come back to our body and our breath and start again. When we do this, we activate neural networks on the sides of our brain that support the sense of letting things be as they are. The neural activity in our midbrain that enables rumination tends to quieten down.

Noticing your reaction, coming back to listening. Drifting off, coming back to your body and breath. Whether it happens once or hundreds of times, it's all OK. Meditation is about the coming back.

When a feeling is challenging, the work of mindfulness is simply to be with it, accepting it as it is (without reactive judgment) and discerning whether a response is needed or not. If you decide to respond and this comes from a calm mind, your response is more skilful. As a leader, parent, partner, friend, it can make all the difference.

———————

There are two ways into mindfulness: secular and spiritual. The secular approach uses mindfulness as a methodology for being more present and having greater balance and more peace in one's life, whereas Buddhists understand mindfulness as a methodology for wisdom, awakening and enlightenment. Both are helpful. Personally, I've found the opportunity offered by the spiritual path for deepening my understanding of myself, others and the world profoundly enriching. Part of that is being open to the impermanent nature of things and realizing that holding onto – 'grasping' – that which, by its very nature, will change, is the cause of much of our suffering.

American vipassana[7] teacher Joseph Goldstein puts it this way:

> The experience of the mind when it's grasping is like rope burn. If you're holding onto a rope that is being forcibly pulled through your hand, you're going to get rope burn. Well, our life is being pulled. It's just a flow completely outside of our ability to stop that flow. Life is change. If we hold on tightly, there's going to be suffering – rope burn. If we learn to go with it, we go with the flow of life.

This doesn't mean being complacent or saying, "there's no point." It means really inhabiting our lives: smelling our cup of tea or coffee before we taste it, then tasting it fully; opening all our senses to our present experience. The force of our awareness connects us to the abundance of life. With mindfulness, the distortions that keep us trapped in our mind gradually dissolve. Through our own observation, we clear the way to understanding who we truly are and what we're capable of.

This is the power of listening inside, mindfully.

All of it, says Sharon Salzberg, is a training in "cultivating greater centeredness, more settledness in our minds, our bodies, our being."

GETTING COMFORTABLE WITH SILENCE

By silence, I mean periods of personal quietude where you are simply with yourself.

The challenge for many leaders is that silence doesn't feel immediately productive. The culture of work doesn't inherently support it. And yet, just as getting to know someone else comes from spending quiet time with them, getting to know yourself comes from spending quiet time with you. If you're ever to find out who and what you are, this is the way.

As my friend and collaborator Christina Kisley says, "If you don't lose some of the noise, you don't even know what's in there."

For those of us living in an urban environment, there's always noise. Vehicles passing, voices speaking, music playing, phones ringing or pinging, footsteps pounding. Alone, we usually turn on some form of sound. With others, we invariably talk. It feels odd not to. We're not used to silence.

But in the noise of life, it's easy to lose ourselves. In the silence, we can reconnect.

For some of us, silence means sitting with that mean person in our head whose voice we normally prefer to drown out. In the silence, we uncover the stories we tell ourselves about ourselves. Then the personal quietude is an act of courage. We're choosing to be present in our own life, to face it as it is, instead of busying ourselves doing anything but.

As a leader, parent, partner, friend, the more you accept yourself as you are, the less judgmental you are of others. The better you know yourself, the easier it is to make the right decisions. The more time you spend holding space for yourself, the easier it is to hold space for others.

Everything begins with us. Being us. As we are. True leadership begins here.

In Erling Kagge's book *Silence: In the Age of Noise*, he describes a moment in 1990, the day after he and fellow Norwegian explorer Børge Ousland reached the North Pole, when an American spy plane flying overhead circled back and dropped a box of food.

They had walked for 58 days in temperatures down to -57°C. Most of their body fat and muscle had burned off. They were truly famished.

The two men divided the food between them – sandwiches, juice and herring – and Kagge was just about to devour his when Ousland suggested they should instead pause for a moment, in silence – "Show collective restraint. Remind each other that satisfaction is also a matter of sacrifice."

"Waiting felt strange," Kagge wrote. "But I have never felt as rich as I did in that moment of silence."

Here, the silence has a quality of inner mastery: of slowing down and becoming more present. Without the moment of silence, they wouldn't have felt as rich.

———————

On a visit to Rome many years ago I joined a public tour of the Vatican. Crowded into the Sistine Chapel with hundreds of others, we weren't allowed to speak. This was enforced by guards belting out "shhh" at regular intervals. In between their shushing, the sound of people murmuring would gradually get louder and louder, until the guards shushed us again.

What if we'd resisted the urge to talk, looked up at the extraordinary, frescoed ceiling, and simply marvelled in silence at Michelangelo's wondrous art? How would that have changed our experience?

———————

Twice a year, when our eight evolving leaders come here to the French Alps on retreat, we spend a day hiking together in the mountains. The space is vast, the landscape magnificent. A perfect moment to be silent. And yet, left to their own devices, the leaders fall into chatter – talking openly and freely about whatever feels important to them at the time.

I'm not suggesting there's anything wrong with that. Talking as you walk with friends in nature is a nice thing to do. But when our hearts and minds are full of noise, we may be missing something.

In my role as their guide, at some point along the way I usually intervene and invite everyone to walk in silence for a while. This lasts for a few minutes, until someone can't resist the urge to share something. Slowly the chatter starts up again.

After a while I pick a spot, a small clearing, and invite them to find their own space. I suggest they make themselves comfortable and be there quietly alone for a few minutes, simply looking at the mountains surrounding us. Then the silence changes. It has an effortless quality. We are sitting before something greater than ourselves. Time seems to slow down.

In this experience, in the hearts and minds of everyone there, something shifts. It's usually hard to express in words, but the sense of shared calm and peace is palpable.

On Erling Kagge's solo expedition to the South Pole in late 1992, for 50 days he encountered no other living creature and no human noise except the sounds he made himself.

"The quieter I became," he writes, "the more I heard."

There are many ways of being silent: a momentary pause; a few minutes of quiet contemplation; a longer sitting meditation; a walk or run in nature; wild swimming. In all of these, you're training your attention to listen for what's there. This supports your capacity to be more present in any circumstance.

———————————

Pausing, listening inside and getting comfortable with silence give you the space you need to discover who you are.

With Mindful Command, you can align who you are with how you lead.

I'm now going to walk you through the four foundations of Mindful Command, with examples of how they work in practice.

CHAPTER FOUR

BALANCED AWARENESS: SEEING THINGS AS THEY ARE

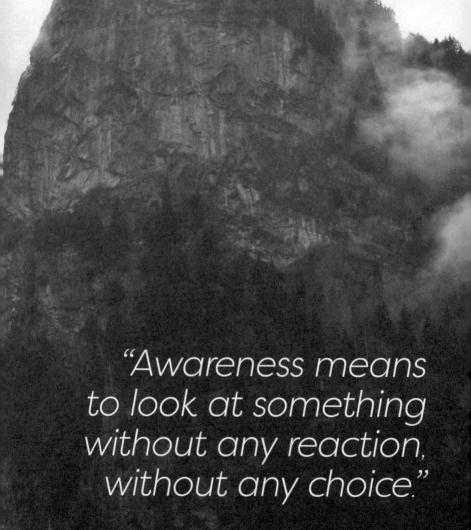

"Awareness means
to look at something
without any reaction,
without any choice."

JIDDU KRISHNAMURTI

When I was 16 living in England, my parents treated us to a long weekend in London. We travelled up from the West Country by train, stayed in a hotel, ate out, went to the theatre, rowed on the Serpentine in Hyde Park, and visited museums and art galleries. One of those was the Tate Britain.

There was an exhibition my father wanted us to see. I've forgotten the artist's name, but I remember the paintings: they were all white painted canvas with an occasional dot. I remember my sister and I looking at them and laughing, wondering how that could be called art.

My father was watching us quietly. After a while he called us over to the other side of the room and pointed to a simple triangular shadow on the wall.

"Things don't always have to mean something," he said calmly. "They can just be there for you to see."

Just there for us to see. "How about that!" cried my 16-year old self.

This was the moment that changed how I look at things.

———————————

I have since come to understand awareness as being like a vast field all around us, full of everything we could ever perceive through our senses. We're in the field, and we're also integral to the field. In Mindful Command, becoming more aware is about perceiving more within us and around us than we have before.

Being aware of someone or something is being open and receptive to the person or the thing as they are. In our busy lives much can obstruct this: not only the matter at hand but also all the nuances, sensibilities and personal agendas associated with normal human behaviour. And things never happen in isolation – they occur during something else, with no definitive beginning or end.

All this creates a kind of mental and emotional turbulence inside us that can prevent us being open and receptive to what is here, now. There's an abiding risk that we see something which is *not* here and miss what *is*.

As a leader, parent, partner, friend, you owe it to everyone concerned to be present and impartial: as best as you can to see things as they are. I call this 'balanced awareness.' It has three key touchpoints: oneself, other(s) and context.

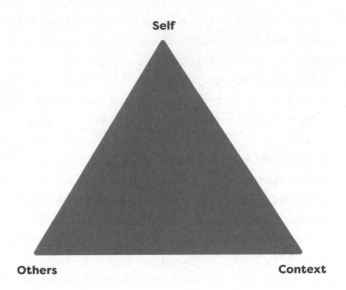

In any situation involving an event and people, these three perspectives are key. Each one needs your equal, unbiased attention. This means seeing not through the lens of our immediate subjective experience (which is bound to be biased) but through the unfiltered eyes of an independent observer.

So, in this three-dimensional view of the same model there is a fourth perspective: you as impartial observer.

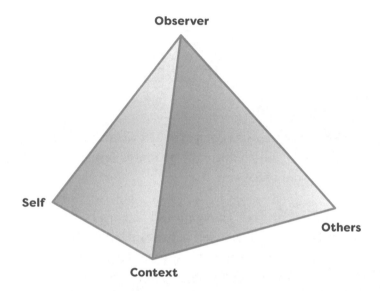

Being the observer requires you to pause, step back, calm your mind and look objectively at each perspective in turn.

AWARENESS
OF SELF

Self-awareness has two parts. The first is noticing your thoughts and feelings, the second is not letting them drive your behaviour.

Tuning into your thoughts and feelings helps you see and understand yourself better and builds your capacity to observe them as they arise. This is the groundwork I describe in the last chapter. Pausing, listening inside, spending time in silence and solitude, noticing the physical sensations of the body, all grow your capacity to connect with your inner state as it is. Just as getting to know someone else comes from spending quiet time with them, getting to know yourself comes from spending quiet time with you.

As you tune into your feelings, it can be helpful to name them: "I'm feeling impatient/frustrated/excited/etc." or "I'm noticing impatience/frustration/excitement/ etc. arising within me." When you do this, you're less likely to get lost in the feeling. You observe the feeling, you name it and you come back to the matter at hand.

The more self-aware you are, the more intentional you can be about how you show up.

If your self-awareness is low, as mine once was, you can also learn a lot by seeing yourself as others do. Sometimes this can be revealed in a 'moment of truth' which comes as a hard knock. This first happened to me as a young adult.

It was my first year at university. One evening I came back to my student accommodation earlier than expected. As I entered my room, I became aware of voices in the room opposite. Then I heard my name. The students I lived with were discussing my weirdness.

I was a thinker and mainly introverted. Coming straight from an all-girls grammar school, my life until then had been relatively sheltered. My way of being was different to most of the people around me, and I'd chosen this progressive university intentionally to broaden my experience.

Hearing them talking about me in that way was difficult, but I kept my bedroom door open and continued to listen. From their perspective, none of what they were saying was untrue. Harsh and unbalanced, but not untrue.

After a while, one of the girls came out to use the bathroom. On her way back, she saw me sitting there and came in. She was visibly concerned and offered a few words of explanation. Then she returned to the other room and brought them all back with her to mine.

What happened then was a frank conversation. They told me things about me I was unaware of. We asked each other questions. We all shed some tears. Gradually, I saw what they were seeing.

Looking back, I think the reason this ended well – painful as it was – is because I was open to listening and curious to understand their perspective. This encouraged them to be open and curious too. The experience helped us see each other. I accepted their feedback and gained new insight. Then I started doing some things differently.

———————————

In my work with leaders, a regular starting point is a piece of feedback they've received at work that makes no sense to them. For example, directors aspiring to board positions are often told to work on their presence and impact. Few see themselves clearly enough to know where to begin.

To ease ourselves into our work together, we might start with their psychometric evaluations and latest 360-degree feedback. These and their strengths, beliefs and values shed some light on their leadership. More important though is their awareness of how they show up: how they see themselves, what they notice in their interactions with others, how these change in different contexts, and what they notice within themselves mentally, physically and emotionally.

Together we explore and expand their capacity to tune into how they're thinking, feeling and holding their body, and how skilfully they can adapt their thoughts, feelings and physical posture in any moment.

This is self-awareness in action: grounding yourself in the moment; becoming aware of your inner self; realizing you're not your thoughts but the one noticing them; and deciding how to act. Every time you pause, turn your attention inwards, breathe and connect, you're building this capacity within you.

Just one minute of grounded attention can make all the difference. I recommend pausing often, at different times throughout your day: in moments of transition; before starting work; between one meeting and the next; on the journey home from work or, if you work from home, before switching to evening activities with your family; and during the night, to quieten unwelcome rumination.

When you do this, you're calming your nervous system, building your connection to you, and creating space to see yourself more clearly. I share more ways of doing this in the final chapter "Standing Calmly for What Matters."

"The quality of our relationships determines the quality of our lives."

ESTHER PEREL

AWARENESS OF OTHERS

In the balanced awareness model, awareness of others is about seeing their perspective clearly, without prejudice. The better you know and understand them, the easier that is.

You can learn a lot about others by observing and listening to them with intention and attention. Your intention is to be open and curious; and you listen with the kind of attention that enables you to see and hear what they're saying and not saying, and their tone of voice, emotions and body language. You notice yourself judging their impact and renew your intention to stay open and curious.

When you listen with intention and attention, you not only listen to what the other person is saying; you're also aware of the thoughts and feelings it triggers in you. You're aware of them, but you don't act on them. This is a skill, and again the pause tool is a key enabler. Sitting quietly, breathing into your centre, you calm your urge to jump in. You stay curious, you keep listening, and you hold space for the other person to speak freely.

As a leader, parent, partner, friend, whether you're listening to learn, to understand, or to allow someone else to work through their own problems, listening with intention signals that you see the other person and care about what they say.

To paraphrase eminent psychologist Carl Rogers, to communicate well we must first listen: "Man's inability to communicate is a result of his failure to listen effectively."

You can also ask others for feedback on what they see in you: when you're skilful and not skilful, and where they notice your impact most and least. This might take the form of formal 360-degree feedback within your organization, or informally asking your peers and individuals in your team how they experience your leadership, or simply asking your close family and friends how they see you.

Listening carefully to what they tell you offers another window into how they think, what matters to them and more. And because you're listening to them, they're more likely to listen to you. You're building connection and trust.

This groundwork helps you look at others not as a potential obstacle but as a team of collaborators, all with their own valuable perspective. You may not agree with some of them, but you see them as they are, and you work with that.

———————

For Michael, a young entrepreneur, the balanced awareness triangle was a reminder to step back and listen, not step in and fix. As the co-founder of a tech start-up, fixing things was his default. He could see this was not a helpful way of enabling his young team to learn and grow, but it was hard for him to change his lifetime habit.

He first noticed a shift during the hectic morning routine with his young children. "When my body is active and my mental activity is light, I can feel the triggers and adapt," he told me. "But when I'm in a work situation just using my mind, it takes me longer."

He described a recent situation where a colleague had brought him a problem with a long rambling back-story. Michael had quickly lost patience and stepped in, keen to guide the conversation to a speedy resolution. "It took me 20 minutes to realize: how am I helping?"

"What got you there?" I asked.

"I think I suddenly saw myself making it all about me. I wasn't listening to him or what he needed. It hadn't even occurred to me to ask what he thought we should do."

This was such a useful insight.

"I've been looking at the triangle through my own eyes," he added, "I think I need to be more objective."

Michael realized that he'd been looking at others through the lens of "mine is the best way to do things." This had got in the way of everything that comes from simply listening to another person expressing what they need to say. By keeping himself quiet, he could allow others to speak. By not solving, he could let others solve, make mistakes, learn and grow.

"This, after all, is a leader's primary role," he concluded.

All this came from Michael's own work on himself. He'd spent long enough reflecting on the triangle of balanced awareness for it to make a strong mental impression. He was also pausing regularly, and this was helping him feel more connected and present. Even at work "just using his mind," he was more in his body than he realized. It was then only a small step to the moment where he asked himself, for the first time, in mid-flow, "how am I helping?"

It turned out to be the first time of many.

This is the value of any practice: one day the thing you're practising just clicks into place – usually when you least expect it.

AWARENESS OF CONTEXT

Context is everything: yes. What's right in one context is wrong in another: yes.

Context is also rather like a Matryoshka doll: dolls within a doll that separate at the middle and reveal a smaller figure of the same kind inside. In other words, context has multiple interconnecting layers, shaped by their scale, scope and complexity.

In the balanced awareness model, awareness of context is having a realistic view of all the layers and their relationship to the matter at hand.

For example, as a parent in conversation with your teenage daughter or son about the uncharacteristically poor quality of their schoolwork, you know this is not going to be a quick fix. There's more to it than meets the eye and you'd like to understand the context better. So, you approach the conversation with an open, curious mind and listen well.

Or, in the same conversation about the poor schoolwork, you allow your expectations and disappointment to be in the driving seat. You demand they tell you why their schoolwork has deteriorated. You set a deadline for improvement and withdraw some privilege until they do.

In the first scenario, you're seeking a realistic solution by endeavouring to understand the broader context and how it may relate to the schoolwork issue. In the second, you're trying to fix the problem without a realistic understanding of all its moving parts.

In your work role, the same principle applies. As a leader responsible, say, for maintaining strategic direction and operational efficiency at a time of continual change, you need to shape priorities and objectives in ways that enable people to feel part of the solution.

However, balancing all your priorities all the time is a big ask of yourself. In moments where it all feels too much, remember the value of pausing. Grab a piece of paper, draw a triangle, focus on the three perspectives, and take stock of who and what is involved. Ask yourself how you're feeling (self), how others are feeling (others) and what is most needed (context).

What makes a challenging situation worse is when leaders forget to do this.

THE IMPARTIAL OBSERVER

Maintaining a realistic view requires a cool head.

As the impartial observer your intention is to be neutral and objective. This doesn't mean you're disinterested in what's happening or how people feel about it. On the contrary, to see things as they are, you must be able to tune into the complexities, sensibilities and nuances of the situation; but not allow them to draw you in and skew your perspective.

Seeing clearly enough to make the best decision for everyone and everything concerned requires you to stay both connected and impartial. A powerful way of doing this is through the quality of your conversations. Make every conversation count by bringing your clear intention and unbiased attention. See the person as they are, listen without judgment and seek to gain a better understanding of what's at play.

If you're currently grappling with something, as most leaders are, call it to mind and try this:

Imagine yourself as an impartial observer, surveying the scene.

How are you feeling?
What is at stake for you?
Who else is involved?
What is at stake for them?
What is this all about?
What are the issues at stake?

Create the space you need for this.
Get up and walk around. Go outside if you can. Take a longer walk. Go for a run or a swim. Journal. Do whatever supports your capacity to look more broadly at what is happening.

When you are ready to, ask yourself:

What is the best realistic outcome?
What is needed to engage others
(your team? key stakeholders? your family?)
to achieve it?

BALANCED AWARENESS IN PRACTICE

In 1998, while still in the Navy I was appointed to the Defence School of Languages (DSL) to teach French. It was outside my mainstream work, and I imagined a couple of non-taxing years for which I felt more than ready. I couldn't have been more wrong.

DSL provided in-house language training in seven key languages to people across the Defence organization. For more than ten years, however, it had been under threat of closure. With that came chronic underfunding, decaying infrastructure, low morale among the largely civilian multinational staff, and a pervading feeling of mistrust and uncertainty.

The real reason I was there soon became obvious. Not to teach French, although I managed to do some of that, but to help restore a sense of identity and worth. I was back in a leadership role.

Looking at the situation through the lens of balanced awareness, here's an overview of what was at play:

- Self: my belief in the value of the school's work, and my desire to give the current students the best possible language learning experience.

- Others: the wellbeing and aspirations of the staff, and the expectations of the customers (the students' sponsors).

- Context: doing the work within the current budget and identifying the most cost-effective solution for defence language training in the future.

In parallel, there were two major external forces:

- The UK government's public-private partnership (PPP) initiative, for which we spent months working on a proposal.

- A UK Ministry of Defence (MOD) Training Review, which then supplanted the PPP project, aiming to rationalize all common training across the three services. When the MOD study team arrived with the premise that all defence language training should be outsourced to the private sector, we saw it as our duty to ensure they had the full facts before deciding. That took two years.[8]

It was a period of continual disruption. There was no business as usual. And yet there were all the usual challenges of managing any underfunded, multicultural, adult-learning institution day to day. It was all about keeping the right balance between the strategic thinking work and the immediate need to improve morale, raise performance standards, build DSL's reputation, and increase its attractiveness to customers and potential new partners.

Keeping a balanced view of everything at stake helped us identify one simple thing we *could* do early on to help turn things around. We invested in a high-quality sign with the full name of the school, which we erected at the entrance from the public road, where previously there had been none. Every morning, as people arrived for work, they were reminded that they were part of something that still mattered.

———————————

As a leader you're always juggling balls, trying to solve problems, and doing your best for everyone and everything concerned. The higher the stakes, the greater the risks and the tougher the decisions required. Mistakes are inevitable. With a balanced perspective you can take them in your stride; and you can pause for long enough to remember what matters most.

CHAPTER FIVE

CLEAR PURPOSE: BEING CLEAR ABOUT WHAT MATTERS

"If you're not clear,
you can do harm."

SARAH METCALFE

Moving with my partner and two young sons to Kyiv in 2005 was not the adventure I thought it would be. It could have been, if I'd formed a clear idea of what the move meant to me personally. Instead, for a long while I floundered.

Just six months earlier, I'd ended my 23-year Navy career. My 16 years of marriage were over too. These two decisions felt necessary, but they were hard to make. The aftershock left me rudderless.

I arrived in Kyiv with no clear idea of what I was doing and why. We were there for my partner's work, and I was what is known as a 'trailing spouse.' This was supposed to be an opportunity for less work, more leisure and time to allow the upheavals of the previous year to settle. But that is not how it turned out for me.

For the first 45 years of my life my purpose had been carved out for me: work hard, be your best, achieve and wear the uniform of service. And now suddenly I was purposeless, and it hit me hard. Disorientated, destabilized, lost, I was grasping at things outside myself. These feelings were new to me, and I didn't know what to do with them.

What I needed at the time was rest and recovery, but instead of taking it easy I looked for things to do. I became a governor and then the business manager of my sons' international school. Getting things done was what I knew how to do. It was also a lot easier than facing my feelings.

Eventually, many different things led me to realize that feeling lost was normal: we all feel lost at times. It was a horrible place to be emotionally, but there was a way through. First, I had to understand that my purpose wasn't 'out there,' it was 'in here.' I needed to stop doing and start listening inside. The answers were already there, waiting for me to ask the right questions.

———————

Clarity is the first principle of leadership. The question "Am I clear?" is the most important of all and the cost of not being clear can have both immediate and long-term impact. Without clarity, you may well keep on doing the wrong things in the wrong way for the wrong reasons. And you may not find your purpose – in other words, the difference you want to make.

The clear answer to any question, big and small, lies somewhere between your head, your heart and your gut. If you listen carefully, you will find it. If you don't, you almost certainly won't.

For example, you're considering where to go on holiday and someone says, "Arcadia is nice," and something inside you says, no, that doesn't feel right. But you go anyway, and you don't like it; and then you wish you'd listened to that feeling.

Or you're in transition and trying to figure out what to do next. Rather than getting clear on what you really want from work, you accept the first good-looking job offer. A few weeks into your new role, you realize it's not where you want to be at all.

When I was introduced to Charles Davies' Very Clear Ideas work, it was immediately obvious to me that his rigorous process offered a reliable path to an idea that's so clear, it leaves you in no doubt.

In the early stages of our Evolving Leadership programme, we introduce the group of eight leaders to Charlie's way of finding reliable paths through challenging feelings and satisfying answers to big questions. We invite them to bring some unclear ideas to work on, both big and small: their life's work, where they want to be at the end of the programme, where to go on holiday that year – dreams, ambitions, frustrations, confusions.

Charlie teaches them his process and they practise it individually and together throughout the programme, until asking themselves "Am I clear?" becomes a habit for life. In practical terms, this often boils down to having the clarity to do what is *needed*, rather than what feels urgent, or is expected, or is easiest.

———————

A very clear idea shows you what matters. Whether that's your family, your career, your community, the environment, achieving life balance, or something else.

For Clare, a senior leader in an organizational role that she'd built from nothing, it clarified her purpose.

Clare was considering stepping away from her career for a while. But something was holding her back. She felt torn. She couldn't quite commit to the idea. On the one hand she wanted to go and find out who she was outside work; and on the other she didn't want to abandon her colleagues and her team. She loved her work, but for many years it had consumed her. Now in her thirties, she was reassessing what mattered to her, and she needed space to reset who and how she wanted to be.

"So many things are up in the air," Clare told me.

When we're unclear, things feel scattered. We want to pin them down, but we have nothing to pin them to. For this feeling to settle, we must pause and get clear.

"I'm scared of feeling lost and unmoored," she added.

"And how do you feel right now?" I asked.

"Lost and unmoored."

She was already in the place she feared most. This is what fear of an imagined future does: it gives life to the fear in the present.

So, I asked her to imagine herself already on her sabbatical and to bring her full attention to already being there. Then I asked her the seven questions at the core of the Very Clear Ideas process:

> *What do you need?*
> *What do you want?*
> *What do you demand?*
> *What do you love?*
> *What do you wish for?*
> *What do you dream of?*
> *What do you live for?*

As she voiced each answer, I wrote it down. Then I read them aloud. As she listened, new thoughts came to her. I added them in; then I pieced her answers together into a long unwieldy sentence – the beginnings of a clearer idea:

> "Is this what you need?" I asked.

> "Yes."

> "Is this what you want... demand... love...
> wish for... dream of... live for...?"

The answer to these test questions must be 100% "yes." This is a rigorous process; you must be sure. 99% "yes" means "no." When Clare's answer was either a straight "no" or not a straight "yes," I asked the open question again, like this:

Is this what you love? No.

OK. *What do you love?*

And I tweaked the sentence and read it back and repeated the test questions until all Clare's answers were 100% "yes." This was now a very clear idea.

I am taking more ownership of my life and committing 100% to the next stage of my life, by finding out who I am, and by taking the time to connect with myself and others and do the things that feed my soul, and by making space for serendipity and spontaneity to lead to opportunities I never would have planned, and by living for myself and not my obligations.

"I've had these feelings inside I haven't voiced," she said. "If I don't do this now, I'll feel as if I shied away from it."

Clare had validated her why. It was always there – smothered by things which seemed more important but, she now realized, mattered less.

She could also see that her fear of being lost and unmoored was linked to a deeper fear of losing her identity, which she'd tied to her work. The Very Clear Ideas process showed her this was not true. She was so much more.

———

When Coca-Cola's former CEO Brian Dyson was invited years ago to give the commencement speech at the Georgia Tech Institute, he must have thought carefully about how to share the key to a successful working life with the young graduates about to start theirs. His key message was that life is a game in which you're juggling five balls: work, family, health, friends and spirit.

> You will soon understand that work is a rubber ball. If you drop it, it will bounce back. But the other four balls – family, health, friends and spirit – are made of glass. If you drop one of these, they will be irrevocably scuffed, marked, nicked, damaged or even shattered. They will never be the same. You must understand that and strive for balance in your life.

Brian Dyson's commencement speech is one of the most viral of its kind on the web.

If, like many people, you're looking for more balance in your life, you might ask yourself what this tells you about your purpose.

Do you want to live a life where you have time to stop and smell the roses? Maybe this is for the purpose of connecting with nature.

Do you want to create more time for your passions? Maybe this is for the purpose of being a more loving partner and parent.

Do you want to actively stand for what you feel is right? Maybe this is for the purpose of making a positive difference to the world.

Our purpose goes to the heart of what matters to us. And when our purpose is about something bigger than ourselves, it gives our life meaning. In other words, when we get clear on our life purpose, it weaves a thread of meaning through our life that makes sense of it all.

WHEN YOUR PURPOSE PRESENTS ITSELF

Sometimes you uncover your purpose through a process like Very Clear Ideas. You ask all the right questions, and you test your answers until your purpose feels right. And sometimes your purpose can be something you seem to stumble upon, and you 'just know.'

Here is someone else's story, that intersects with my own, and shows how this can happen. I'll tell it as if it were yours...

You're on a family holiday in the French Pyrenees, and you chance upon a remote and abandoned village. You have the beginnings of a vision to rebuild it. One of the derelict buildings catches your eye and you want to buy it. You track down the owner, a local farmer, and agree a price. You spend the rest of your life bringing the vision into being. It changes your life, and your young family's life, forever.

You have two sons. The younger later becomes an entrepreneur, like you. The older eventually takes over the luxury leather goods business you founded in 1934, soon after you left your native Germany and your promising career as a film producer, for a new life in England.

Every summer for many years, with your artist wife and your two sons you work to fulfil your dream. In the first six years you rebuild just enough of your property to be able to live there. Over time you renovate the whole building completely. You bring electricity and running water to the village for the first time, and its former inhabitants gradually return.

You work with love. Your toil is for something greater than the product of your labours. In the decay, you see beauty; in the neglect, you see an opportunity to restore life. And you want to make it right – because you can.

You have a successful life: a thriving business, a good income and a beautiful family. You've travelled widely; you speak five languages; lots of people know and admire you; you've made your mark. And yet there was something else, wasn't there? Something that struck you the moment you saw it; something, perhaps, about building a place that feels like home.

This was your purpose all along. It may have snuck up on you unawares, but it was always there, in your heart. A kind of inner knowing waiting to be heard.

Some 40 years after you found your home, my husband and I found ours. One misty day in the French Alps, we saw it and just knew. Was it the two huge mountains? The flowing river? Or the charm of a big, old, neglected farmhouse? Something was pulling us in.

Of all the steps on the long, winding road of our life, this was to be the most purposeful. For the 12 extraordinary years that the house was ours, it held a vision that we brought to life. Opening our doors to the hundreds of people who passed through – friends, family, skiers, hikers, yogis, adventurers – we gradually realized that our real work was for the people seeking space in their frenzied lives for calm, and time to think. And this is how the Evolving Leadership programme began – in the place we call home.

What threads your story and ours together is this: just weeks after we decided to put our home up for sale the person who came to buy it was your younger son. He too found it – unexpectedly – while on holiday with his family, just as you found yours 50 years before.

This is how I come to know your story. Your home became your purpose, and your purpose your home. The same is true for us. And if you had not found your home, who knows if your son would have found ours. What I do know is that we sold our home to the right people.

So, thank you. You may no longer be with us in person, but your purpose lives on in the lives of the people it has touched.

I invite you, the reader, to pause for a moment.

Is there someone you know whose purpose has touched you?

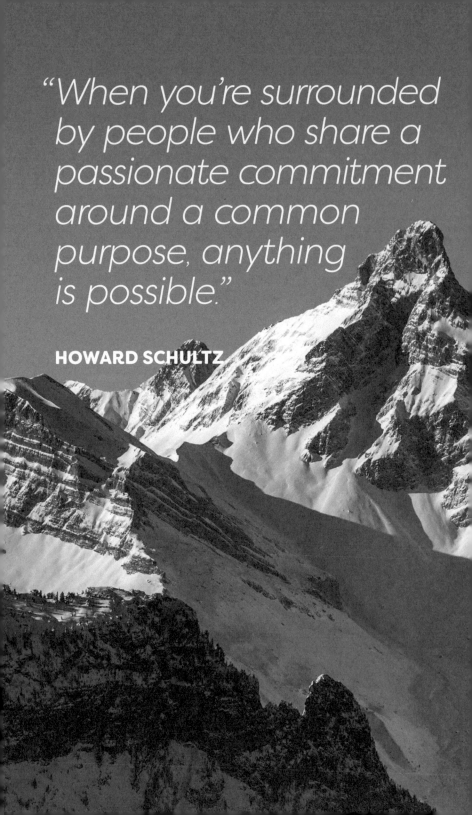

"When you're surrounded by people who share a passionate commitment around a common purpose, anything is possible."

HOWARD SCHULTZ

WHERE PURPOSE IS SHARED

In leadership, a purpose is only clear when it makes sense to everyone involved. In the context of Mindful Command, a shared clear purpose needs to embody both clarity and balanced awareness. Clarity is the first principle of leadership, and balanced awareness expands your field of view. Together they broaden your capacity to see what matters. And this is where shared clear purpose begins.

When people working together have the same view of the difference they want to make, they generate a shared purpose. In any context, a clear shared purpose helps people overcome difficulty and find mutually beneficial solutions. It drives better outcomes.

The leader's role is to create the conditions for clear, purposeful work. To do this, you must be clear about what matters to you, understand what matters to the people you lead, and keep a balanced awareness of the twists and turns of your collective context.

For a purpose to be truly shared, it needs to be built together and tested once complete. It must be simple, clear and 'ring true,' and everyone involved must find meaning in it. Otherwise, their commitment to it will be half-hearted.

When someone in your team is only partially committed to the team purpose, it usually means it doesn't ring true for them. To test this gently, you could ask them to read the purpose out loud as if they really mean it, and then ask them:

> *Does it feel right?* No.
>
> OK. *What's in it that shouldn't be?*
> *And what's missing?*

This can work well as a team exercise in which people ask each other the question in pairs and revise the purpose statement until they both agree on it. Each pair pins their version to a board, and everyone reads all the versions and ticks the one they like best. You read out the one with the most ticks and test it again with the whole team.

The added value here – as well as determining a truly shared purpose – is in everyone speaking openly to each other about what feels right to them. It strengthens relationships and unifies the team around the purpose of their work. The time it takes is always worth it. As the team leader, this teamwork on your team purpose is one of the most important reasons you're there.

In the autumn of 1990, the command team of Royal Navy frigate HMS *London* understood this well.

A few weeks earlier, the world had been stunned by Iraq's full-scale invasion of Kuwait and subsequent disregard for the United Nations Security Council's unanimous demand to withdraw. HMS *London* had been ready to deploy to the Middle East as a routine Navy presence, safeguarding British shipping in the Gulf.[9] Now the ship was to go to war. It had to be prepared for the very specific threat that Iraq wouldn't hesitate to use both chemical weapons and its known stock of Exocet anti-ship missiles.

HMS *London* was already in a state of high operational readiness, but, as the ship steamed east, its leaders' focus was firmly on the additional measures necessary to ensure the ship and the crew were completely prepared for what was to come. The Navy's top operational trainers were embarked to put the crew through their paces again and again, particularly with respect to operating in a chemical environment. And, from the moment the ship arrived in the Gulf, three months before the start of the conflict, the crew went straight into the defence watches (six hours on, six hours off) necessary to operate a ship at war. In other words, the leaders were very clear about what mattered.

The allied operation involved 35 nations. Their shared purpose[10] was to liberate Kuwait, restore its legitimate government and stabilize Middle East oil supplies.

For the 18-nation naval coalition the shared purpose was to establish and maintain command of the sea.

For all the ships, including HMS *London*, the shared purpose was to defend against all threats, contribute to the coalition's offensive effort and maintain the safety of everyone on board.

And for the people on board the shared purpose was to be at their peak of individual and team capability so that they had the best possible chance of protecting the people and the things they loved.

In a complex conflict with much at stake, the purpose needs to be both abundantly clear and truly shared. Everyone must buy into the why. The crew of HMS

London had to be as one, and the top priority of the command team was to invest the time and effort necessary to keep that intact. This meant that the shared purpose had to be visibly executed.

More than inspiring words, this needed focused, practical measures. For example: clearly communicating the ship's objectives and all developments as they occurred; maintaining team spirit and confidence with daily skills training, including with other ships in the naval coalition; going the extra mile to enable a clear understanding of the threats and the ship's ability to counter them, including detailed risk analyses, defensive missile firings and mine countermeasures; programming periodic safe replenishments at sea to ensure decent food stocks and mail delivery; emphasizing the value of every individual contribution to the collective effort; and, as important as anything else, maintaining the sense of humour that keeps the human spirit alive.

The ship and its crew survived the war unharmed. As one of its leaders later told me: "It was my strongest sense of purpose ever. When your purpose is that clear, nothing is wasted."

War never feels right. What does feel right is protecting what you love. This gives you a strong enough purpose not just to comply with orders, but to fully commit to what must be done. In an awful situation you have something that matters to hold on to.

When you have a purpose that you can believe in, it carries you through.

———————————

There is nothing like a major crisis to highlight the power of purpose. In a large scale crisis affecting a lot of people, the leader must harness what matters most and articulate its truth for everyone to hear. This forms the clear purpose people can get behind. And it fuels their courage to act.

In the first week after Russia's 2022 full-scale invasion of Ukraine, on the street in his threatened capital, surrounded by advisers and members of his cabinet, President Zelensky held his mobile phone out in front of him and spoke these words to his people:

> *I'm here, we're here, we're not going
> anywhere, we're going to stand here
> together, to defend our homes,
> families, children.*

As I write, the war rages still. He has spoken to the nation every evening since and the unified spirit his leadership has engendered is undoubtedly the nation's greatest defence.

Not only have people come forward in their masses to fight, but they have also driven into besieged cities to evacuate civilians, delivered supplies to the front line, cooked food for combat troops, and worked around the clock to keep all essential services running – hospitals, electric power, mobile phone networks, fire and rescue – against all the odds.

If ever proof were needed that leadership has nothing to do with role, position or stature, and everything to do with clarity, courage and presence, then this president is a resounding example.

From the very first moment of taking up office his purpose was clear: "Don't hang photos of me in your offices," he told parliament, "Hang photos of your children instead." He was very clear about that then, and this is what guides him now.

———————————

To many, Volodymyr Zelensky is a hero. Yes. He's also a human being who is very clear about what matters.

We can all be that. And we don't need to experience a life-and-death situation to do it.

In the words of leadership professor and author, David Burkus:

> While modern corporations spend billions
> of dollars every year on 'team building' and
> on making sure that they hire top talent to
> 'get the right people on this bus,' it turns out

there is a much older, and much lower cost, way to rally a team. It's not about ropes courses, trust falls, or any other of the team building activities that so many have tried and found wanting. It's not even about how to motivate people by casting a vision or setting a big hairy audacious goal.

It's about finding out, or sometimes just declaring, what battle your team is fighting. It's about finding the common threat to the team or its stakeholders and outlining a clear path to overcoming it.

In other words, whatever the context, whatever your role, your job as a leader is to unite your people around what matters most and manifest the clear, shared purpose they need to be their best.

And remember, this starts with you.

CHAPTER SIX

FEARLESS COMPASSION: CULTIVATING THE COURAGE TO DO THE RIGHT THING

"When we understand that we cannot be destroyed, we are liberated from fear."

THICH NHAT HANH

In Mindful Command, fearless compassion is about embracing fear with compassion and thereby cultivating the courage to do the right thing.

**When the hand of compassion
meets the hand of fear,
there is courage.**

This is the opposite of ignoring your fear and pushing on through. Instead, you acknowledge your fear and explore its impact on you and your choices. Fear is hard, but hard doesn't mean bad. When you lean into your fear with a compassionate, enquiring mind, you gain a better understanding of things as they are – and not as they are when distorted by fear.

Acting with fearless compassion is not a quick fix, but the rewards are greater self-understanding, better decision-making and better relationships.

You are happier, and so are the people you lead and love.

———————————

Any of us living or working in a city almost anywhere in the world cannot walk the streets of that city without seeing people who have made the streets their home. Some out of choice perhaps, but most not. How do we feel about that? What, if anything, do we do?

I am going to explore just one of many possible scenarios. As you read on, I invite you to notice what you think and feel.

My friend Tom is a working parent living in a large city. On his way to the grocery store one evening, at the end of a long day, he sees a woman and four children sitting by the side of the road. The woman is holding a sign with the words "PLEASE HELP FEED MY FAMILY."

Tom stops. He asks the woman what she needs and realizes she hasn't understood the question. One of the children – the eldest, Tom thinks – explains in broken English that they have been given a place to stay, but not enough to eat. Tom asks them what they like to eat and walks on. A little while later he comes back with food to last them a few days. He also gives them a grocery store token for later. Then he goes home.

In this situation there is no rule book. There is no one way. There is only what we – you, me and Tom – feel is right. We can walk on by, or we can stop. If we stop, we can give money, buy them a drink or food, have a conversation, donate to a suitable charity, do something else or do nothing. The factors influencing our choice may be personal: like our values and beliefs, which influence, for example, our view of whether people 'deserve' our help or not. Or they may be practical, like how much time and money we have. Or they may be directly driven by something more deeply human, like compassion or fear.

All this, and more, influences what you do in the moment: whether you turn toward or turn away from the difficulty facing you, whatever it may be.

For Tom, the biggest challenge is his fear of getting involved. He doesn't trust his own boundaries. He's afraid of getting drawn in, being duped, being taken advantage of and in the end doing more harm than good. Whatever he does, he always feels he could have done more, and this painful feeling stays with him for days to come.

"I feel so torn," he said. "I wrestle with it all the time."

Tom's desire to relieve suffering – his compassion – is constrained by his fear of some kind of negative consequence. Compassion and fear are like opposing forces residing within him: one, clear and connected, urging him forward; the other, fear-based, pulling him back.

Within Tom, within every one of us, is a human being struggling to find their way. Our struggle is our relationship with our own inner obstacles, many of which are borne of unconscious fear.

EXPLORING FEAR

Fear has many forms. Common to many leaders I work with, is an unconscious fear of failure, of inadequacy, or of rejection; and these can show up emotionally as anxiety, self-doubt, frustration, anger and more. Fear is deeply personal; we all experience it differently. What triggers one person's fear of failure, for example, may only register to another person as a minor blip. What matters is that we acknowledge our own fears and understand their impact on us and the people around us.

In the words of writer and vipassana teacher Jack Kornfield: "Although most of us have been deeply conditioned by fear, for the most part we have avoided directly exploring its nature. Because we are not aware of its workings, it is often an unconscious driving force in our lives."

Research in the field suggests that we're all born with a fear of falling and a fear of sudden loud noises. All other fears are learned through our experience of life. They lodge themselves in our emotional memory and get hard-wired into our nervous system, becoming part of who we are.

As a child I loved dogs. I still do, but at times I'm also afraid of them. I can trace this back to a day over 50 years ago when as a young girl I was visiting a neighbouring farmer. We knew him well and I was walking through his front yard past his sheep dogs in the same way I had many times before. That day though, one of the dogs approached me silently from behind and without warning bit deep into the back of my leg. The fear that gripped me soon after that attack has never left me. Today, when I'm out walking and see a dog off the leash, I feel the fear again, rising in my belly and gripping my chest and throat.

This strong physical reaction is my amygdala at work: matching the event to the emotional memory it captured and stored all those years ago. The split second I see the dog, my amygdala is on full alert, triggering the same fear I felt back then. This "in-the-moment" fear, as sports psychologist and author Dr Pippa Grange calls it, is an unconscious reaction to a perceived threat. My deep survival instinct has kicked in; hundreds of chemicals are being instantaneously released into my body and brain; and my nervous system is transmitting an urgent message to my heart to pump harder to enable the many physiological changes that will prepare my body for action. At the same time my rational capacity is reducing and my field of view narrowing to the point that I can no longer clearly discern what is true and what is not.

In other words, my primeval reactive self is in the driving seat again, not necessarily taking me in the right direction.

Pause for a moment. Lay your hand on your chest or your belly, or one hand on each. Observe your breath entering and leaving your body.

Imagine yourself in an everyday situation where you experience some kind of in-the-moment fear – like mine with the dog.

As you call the situation to mind, notice any physical sensations in your body. Notice your thoughts. And notice how this makes you feel.

Now gently, kindly, ask yourself this: "Do I know for a fact that what I'm telling myself is true?"

In all circumstances where we experience fear, this is a valuable question. Asking it engages the fact-finding part of our mind to explore another perspective. As we entertain the possibility of a different way of looking and seeing, our fear begins to lose its grip.

When I encounter a dog off the leash and feel the same old fear taking hold, this is how I respond:

"Here we are again," I say to myself. And then I look at the dog. What kind of dog is this? What is their demeanour? What are they defending? How threatening are they, really?

Then I say something like, "This is a dog being a dog. It's not the dog's fault I'm afraid." In most cases, there is nothing real to fear.

This kind of in-the-moment risk assessment of my in-the-moment fear is just enough to walk me through it. It helps me see my fear for what it is.

————————

Professional solo sailor Pip Hare expects there to be a moment in every ocean race where she experiences "the dry mouth, elevated heart rate, pounding in my ears, and fight or flight grip of real fear," as her 60-foot IMOCA-class yacht races through the dark ocean, smashing through the waves.

And sure enough, during the Vendée Globe single-handed round the world yacht race such a moment came. In the second half of the non-stop three-month race, the wind instruments at the top of the mast stopped working. Pip and her yacht were safe, but without wind data she lacked the vital information necessary to navigate an optimum course. She would lose the place in the race which she had worked so hard to gain. The only way she could change the instruments was to climb to the top of the mast, 30 metres above sea level.

"I was terrified of climbing the mast. Really, really scared."

Acknowledging her fear, saying it out loud, made the fear less powerful. "It gives me some sort of control, and it feels like a step towards defeating the monsters." She later wrote.

She took stock of everything that could possibly go wrong. "I looked at the negative outcomes square in the face." She saw the many risks in climbing the mast and listed them one by one.

She also assessed the mitigating factors: her training, experience, skill, expertise and expensive top-of-the-range equipment. The weather conditions were perfect too, and the horizon was clear.

In other words, she completed a thorough audit of all relevant factors. The fact-finding part of her mind was speaking truth to fear, ensuring she was making the right decision for the right reasons. However, if this process had been unable to convince her that the worst would not happen, then she would have heeded her fear's warning and done what was needed to protect herself and her boat. "Sometimes fear has a place," she admitted.

Yes. Always. At its core fear is never wrong. Fear shows up to remind us of something that once caused us suffering, or to alert us to something unknown in the future. However, for fear to be helpful it's necessary to see it for what it is, and not for what it at first seems to be.

Once we've done our audit, there are two more important questions to ask: What will happen if I don't do this thing that I'm afraid of? What might I regret?

This was Pip's answer: "I had an opportunity to change this. I had worked so hard to get my place on the start line and I'd battled all the way around the world. I could not live with myself if I took the easy option at that moment. I had to keep fighting, I had to try."

This was personal. Not everyone would feel the same way. You might well find yourself thinking there's no way you'd climb that mast, but for Pip it was worth it. As a leader, parent, partner, friend, only we can know our own limits and only we can truly test and trust them.

Pip knew herself well enough to be in no doubt: if she didn't climb the mast then, she would not be able to live with herself later. Ultimately, this is what generated the courage she needed to master her fear.

Courage is deeper than reason and larger than fear. It's our capacity to listen inside for what is right and then do it. This can take a split second or longer, but deep down we always know.

Pip climbed the mast. She was proud that she did.

Years ago, I was asked to speak at a public event for the first time since leaving the Navy. In the weeks, days, hours and minutes before stepping onto that stage, my anxiety became a sense of overwhelming dread. I could feel it deep in my belly, and I could hear it in my ruminating thoughts, questioning my every move. Looking back, I'm amazed that I somehow managed to stand up there and say what I wanted to. Today my message would be clearer and more succinct, but with hindsight I can see that what I said then was good enough. That's not how it felt at the time though. Then I could only see how much better it could have been.

So, I suffered before, during and after an event which was supposed to be fun. And all because I convinced myself I was not good enough.

In my work with leaders, I see this type of situation frequently. Dr Pippa Grange has seen it a lot too and names it the "not-good-enough" fear. Unlike in-the-moment fear, which is acute and specific, not-good-enough fear is chronic and pervasive.

"When your mind distorts fear into stress about the past or the future – we often call this anxiety," writes Dr Grange in her book, *Fear Less*. "This is fear of what might happen or not happen, and what that means for our survival, whether this is a real threat or not."

Fear is at the root, she says, of all our anxiety-induced negative thoughts and feelings and agitated behaviours – like mine above. She explains:

> When you feel jealousy, at root you'll find a fear of not being lovable. When you get sucked into perfectionism, at root you'll find a fear of failing. When you want to judge people or you feel judged, at root you'll find a fear of inadequacy. When you feel you have to keep yourself separate, at root you'll find your fear of being rejected.

Behind all these fears is our base human fear of not being enough and, therefore, being abandoned. As a human being, you and I fear this more than anything else.

In our young life, particularly as physically helpless babies, our survival depends on others wanting to take care of us. Our desire to survive is thus tied to a fear of being abandoned. We do everything we can to ensure we're worthy of our carer's care. But the fear of not being enough never completely disappears. It's at the root of our fear of loneliness, of being ill, of growing old and of dying.

Whatever form our fear takes, if we can't see what's happening and understand our fear for what it is, it will stand in the way of being the leader, parent, partner, friend we can be.

This is why it's so important to approach your difficult feelings with a compassionate, enquiring mind. A skilled coach, therapist or counsellor can guide you in this, and there are ways you can help yourself.

"Fear is the natural reaction to moving closer to the truth."

PEMA CHÖDRÖN

EXPLORING COMPASSION

Consciously cultivating more compassion in your life is about showing up with less judgment, more curiosity; less telling, more listening; less defensiveness, more open heartedness. Because to live and work together well, this is what we need more of.

To be compassionate is to see people as they are and listen for what they need. It's more than sympathy, where we feel for the person; or empathy, where we feel with them and can relate to their experience. It implies a desire to alleviate another person's suffering. A simple act of compassion might be speaking with kindness, helping someone in difficulty or offering your seat to a person finding it hard to stand.

Sometimes though, we can be so concerned for the needs of others that we forget to take care of our own. Or at least it can feel that way. My friend and collaborator Max St John says this isn't actually true: we always put our own needs first (more on that later). Nevertheless, in moments when we feel totally spent, it can seem as if all our energy has been used up on other people and things.

Pause for a moment. Lay your hand on your
chest or your belly, or one hand on each.
Observe your breath entering and leaving
your body.

Call to mind a time when you felt mentally,
emotionally and/or physically depleted.
(Maybe that time is now.)

How did you respond? What happened?

Did you take a break?
Ease up?
Rest and recover?
Or did you drive yourself harder still?

Among the leaders I work with, the majority are impossibly stretched. Juggling too many balls, they have no space for themselves. With no space for themselves, they lose perspective. With diminished perspective, they lose sight of what matters. And they judge themselves harshly for not being able to do it all. Can you relate?

Reinforcing this is the wider culture of 'self-improvement.' Human beings everywhere are relentlessly striving for more, and in the process feeding their fear of not being enough.

When fear is your driver, you will never be enough.

In this mode of harsh self-judgment, self-compassion is absent. Harsh self-judgment can only cause more harm, whereas self-compassion has the potential to soothe and heal.

There is a well-known Buddhist parable about two arrows. The first arrow causes pain; the second causes suffering. The first arrow is a painful event; the second arrow is how you respond to it. Do you observe the first arrow, learn from it and move on; or do you resent it, blame yourself and worry? If you tend to do the latter, then you're adding a second arrow to the first and making the whole thing worse. It keeps you in what Tara Brach, psychologist, author and meditation teacher, calls the "trance of unworthiness." I call it "the prison of must improve."

In the prison of must improve you judge yourself harshly. Your jaw clenched, you might think or say something like: "This is ridiculous, you should be able to do this." "They're all laughing at you." "You're not young/beautiful/clever enough to be loved."

Whereas, in the freedom of self-compassion you might place your hand on the area around your heart and say: "There, there, sweetheart, it will be OK." "You have the skills; you can do this." "You have everything you need."

From deficiency to sufficiency, simply in the way you talk to yourself. We can all do this. Here are two friendly ways:

Play 'spot the not enough.' This is a game in which you observe yourself being yourself, and notice when you think or say something that makes you less than you are – like "I can't" or "I shouldn't" – or any self-deprecating judgment – like "hopeless" or "I should be able to do this" or "typical of me" – even when you think you're saying them in jest. Every time you spot a not enough, pause and write it down, in your journal if you have one or in a notebook. Be curious about it. You may well find there are things you've been saying to yourself for some time without noticing, and they have stealthily become part of how you see yourself.

Practise mindful breathing. This is pausing and becoming aware of your breathing. Do this at any time but particularly when you're worried about something in the past or anxious about something in the future. Quietly repeat to yourself, "Breathing in, I know I am breathing in; breathing out, I know I am breathing out." Concentrate on your breath. You're simply being with yourself as you are now, in this moment, and allowing your breath to calm your feelings.

In both these ways, you're turning toward yourself and including all the parts of yourself you consider wrong. In the game, you're being curious about yourself; in the practice, you're generating the feeling of mind and body together – a whole you – living not in the past or the future, but now.

The more 'whole' you feel, the less isolated you feel you are from others. Compassion author and academic Dr Kristin Neff puts it this way: "Self-compassion involves recognizing that suffering and personal inadequacy are part of the shared human experience – something that we all go through rather than something that happens to 'me' alone."

As your self-compassion grows, you judge yourself less. You judge others less too. Where you might previously have turned your harsh self-judgment outwards toward others in the form of blame, frustration, anger, you become more understanding of their human foibles.

In other words, the more compassion you have for yourself, the easier it is to have compassion for others. Be your own friend first.

For years, Fiona had doubted herself. Even now, as the head of organizational development in a large UK organization, she would look at leaders who were senior to her and marvel at their skilful management of huge workloads. Marvelling, while also telling herself she would never be able to do that in the way they did.

"Such a huge challenge frightens me," she confided.

Fiona was leading several workstreams. Individually they were manageable, but when she stopped to consider the entire scope of her work, she felt overwhelmed. This diminished her sense of competence and she berated herself for it. To others, she was a good leader doing great work.

"What is the purpose of your work?" I asked her.

"To lead strategic organizational change," she replied, without hesitation.

"So senior leaders hold you to account to deliver on that?"

"Yes."

"And what do you hold yourself to account for?"

Long pause.

"I'm not really sure. I need to develop my own thinking about how the organization needs to change."

"How would you like to do that?"

Tiny pause.

"I need to figure out the trends, and work with others to gain insights and develop ideas."

Fiona knew what to do. Deep behind her fear of failure, she'd always known. And yet her fear of getting things wrong had given her the mistaken idea that she had to get everything right. By 'everything,' she included all the things on her to-do list, whether they needed to be there or not. By 'right,' she'd decided that her opinion only counted when someone else asked for it. She'd, therefore, been keeping her mouth mainly shut. In senior leadership meetings, where her voice was most needed, she had mostly been silent.

She now realized that rather than trying harder in the role, she needed to change her way of seeing her role. "I need to start purposely doing important things," she said.

She decided to become more curious. She paid close attention to how the more experienced directors showed up, what they chose to say and when they chose to say it. In high level meetings, she made a conscious effort to shift her focus away from needing to understand everything, to making more space for the higher level thinking her role required. She also began asking for help and gathering the right people together to brainstorm the key issues.

Gradually, Fiona relaxed into her role. As she did, her overwhelming to-do list became more of an overarching mind map.

"Most challenges have aspects that we may never fully understand," she concluded. "The best we can do is work with things as they are and remember we don't need to do everything at once."

Hear, hear.

HEALTHY CONFLICT

Opening our hearts and minds to our fears and judgments gives us courage to listen compassionately for what is needed in any situation, including where there's conflict.

Conflict is neither good nor bad. It just happens from time to time, as a normal part of living and working together. What makes it healthy or unhealthy is how we respond to it. If we want to, there's always something we can learn. If we avoid it, we miss that opportunity. For conflict to be resolved, its origin needs to be surfaced and understood.

Few people understand this better than my friend and collaborator Max St John. Every year, he brings his wisdom to our Evolving Leadership programme and guides the leaders through a process of exploring their own relationship with conflict and understanding how to respond to it with more skill.

Pause for a moment.

With your journal or notebook to hand, call
to mind a difficult event (not too difficult:
5 on a scale of 1-10) – perhaps a
conversation that didn't go to plan.

What happened? What was the moment
it went wrong?

What feelings and physical sensations
did you notice?

Who did you see as responsible for
what happened?

What did you and they do?

What happened then?

Notice how you feel about the event now. What do you
want to learn from it?

I recommend you capture your reflections in your journal or in a way that works for you.

Everyday conflict at home or at work is usually sparked by words or actions that give rise to difficult feelings, like anxiety, frustration, anger, impatience. We feel aggrieved in some way, and we instantly look for someone to blame, judging them as lazy, mean, selfish and so on. We want the unpleasant experience to go away quickly, and we react in haste. The other person counter-reacts, and the conflict begins, stopping only when someone does something different.

At the heart of this cycle of judgment and blame, says Max, is an unmet need. Unmet needs have an urgency to them. They can be more powerful than fear, pushing you to do things your deepest fears tell you not to. For example:

- You fear rejection but your unmet need for connection is stronger and drives you to join that Salsa class.

- You fear losing your daughter when she leaves home, but your unmet need for a lasting, healthy relationship forces you to release your control on her life.

- You fear feeling guilty about taking time for yourself, but your unmet need to understand yourself better finally persuades you to do it (and the work).

Fear and unmet needs can be deeply rooted and difficult to fathom, and almost impossible to deconstruct.
Remember that someone else's needs are just as important to them as yours are to you. And their fears drive
their behaviour in the same way your fears drive yours.
Remembering this helps us cultivate a more compassionate understanding of what is at stake when conflict occurs.

Max shares a story of what can go wrong when an
everyday need is unmet. You're working from home,
and you feel cold. You have a need for wellbeing (perhaps coming from a fear of not being well enough to do
good work), and you want to meet your need by getting
warm. So, you turn the heating on. But your partner
is at home too and they're not cold, so they ask you to
turn it off. This annoys you: your need for wellbeing
becomes a need for autonomy. You refuse. Your partner
gets upset: "You never listen to me!" Their unmet need
is to be seen and heard (perhaps from a fear of being
worthless). Now you're in a fight. Your original need for
physical wellbeing has been displaced and there is real
risk that you will both say things you later regret.

While this example may seem relatively minor, the
principles characterize all conflict, big or small.
Looking at it through the lens of the twin arrows in
the Buddhist parable, the first arrow (your need for
wellbeing) causes discomfort; the second arrow (your
need for autonomy) is the secondary conflict that
shows up when you perceive your original need for

wellbeing is being blocked. The second arrow goes deeper than the first.

To move through this, one of you must consciously pause. And, difficult though it may be, that person is you. What matters more? Winning this argument or safeguarding your relationship? A way through is to reconnect with your original need and ask yourself if there's an alternative to turning the heating on. Could you put on a sweater? Jog on the spot? Hug your partner?

Getting stuck on one single way, and not being able to see beyond it, causes a kind of 'no way out' thinking on which conflict thrives and escalates.

When we're curious enough, we find there's more than one way of meeting a need.

John, founder and CEO of a small consultancy, had been putting off a difficult conversation with Sam. A key member of his team, she was performing poorly against some key objectives and making life difficult for him and everyone else. This was nothing new: right from her first days on the payroll John had doubted Sam's commitment.

"Every time I try to talk to her about it though," John told me, "she goes on the attack, accusing me of not being fair and telling me I'm causing her stress."

Overworked and overwhelmed, John couldn't see a way through. But he couldn't keep on giving Sam the benefit of the doubt, hoping it would all resolve itself. He knew he had to have a proper conversation with her and was dreading it.

"When you think about having this conversation," I asked him, "what are you afraid of?"

"My biggest fear is that Sam won't listen; she'll misunderstand me, and we won't get anywhere."

"What do you think she's afraid of?"

"That she loses her job?"

"Maybe." I replied. "And what do you think she needs?"

"I don't know."

"What do you need?"

Long pause.

"I need us to have an honest conversation. I want to understand Sam and I want her to understand me."

Acknowledging his fear and his needs reminded John that Sam had fears and needs too. He'd been focusing on her behaviour and its impact, not on the human being behind it.

John scheduled a meeting with Sam and asked her to come to his office. He prepared carefully, establishing the facts and gathering some recent concrete examples – good and bad – of her individual work and her teamwork. In the minutes leading up to the meeting, he made time to gather himself too – pausing, breathing, grounding his body and calming his mind. He set his intention to say only what was necessary and to listen carefully to Sam's response, whatever it may be. He decided that what mattered most in this first conversation was to encourage her to speak truthfully, and for him to seek to understand. He wanted to align on a way forward and set the tone for the conversations to come.

He said things like:

"We're here to talk about..."

"Does that make sense to you?"

"This is how I see it. I understand you may not see it the same way."

"It sounds like you feel..."

"Here is where we have common ground... I want you to grow, and you want to grow..."

"And here is where we disagree..."

And he paused often, resisting the temptation to fill in the blanks and allowing moments of reflective silence. Sometimes it can be helpful to give someone space simply to hear themselves.

In bringing the conversation to a close, John summarized what he'd understood and voiced some reasonable expectations. Sam clarified a few things and then agreed – slightly reluctantly, John thought; but it was a start. They agreed to meet again in a month.

In the words of American football coach Bill O'Brien: "The success of an intervention depends on the interior condition of the intervenor."

When we're stuck – perhaps we're clinging to something and unable to let it go or we're putting something off because it feels too hard – it's worth asking ourselves, "What am I afraid of?"

Ask it kindly. Listen to yourself with compassion. You're exploring the nature of an unconscious force driving your life. This takes courage. It also gives you the courage to do the right thing.

CHAPTER SEVEN

INNER STABILITY: STANDING CALMLY FOR WHAT MATTERS

"The cornerstone of stability is to know that there is nothing wrong with the essential human being"

W. TIMOTHY GALLWEY

Early in my naval career, when I was still finding my feet, I had an irascible boss. One day he vented his anger at me. I remember standing in front of him, motionless, speechless, looking straight back at him. He stopped shouting. And he never shouted at me again.

Afterwards, I wondered what had happened exactly. I had just stood there, apparently unperturbed, and he had stopped shouting. I think he interpreted my delayed reaction as strength.

Quite by chance, I'd discovered the power of standing my ground. I've been exploring it ever since.

———————

Inner stability, the fourth foundation of Mindful Command, is the capacity to stand calmly for what matters to you in the face of uncertainty, volatility or chaos.

Most of us know the feeling of being unstable. Like a ship on rough seas, you feel thrown about. You might experience a kind of inner churning and a sense of separation from yourself and others; and your thinking is scattered.

Pause for a moment. Think about a time
when you felt unstable inside.

What was the situation?
What mattered to you at the time?
What factors contributed to you feeling
unstable inside?
What was the outcome of the situation?

We can probably all think of times when our way of showing up made a difficult situation worse. Can you also remember a time when you faced a difficult situation feeling grounded and centred? Where you felt stable inside and you stayed connected to yourself and others? What was the outcome then?

The four foundations of Mindful Command and the tools and practices that support them develop your capacity to balance your awareness, clarify your purpose, quieten your fear and act compassionately. The clearer, more balanced and more connected you are, the more stable and grounded you feel. And the more stable you feel, the easier it is to balance your awareness, clarify your purpose, quieten your fear and act compassionately.

In the context of Mindful Command, inner stability is both the bedrock and the outcome.

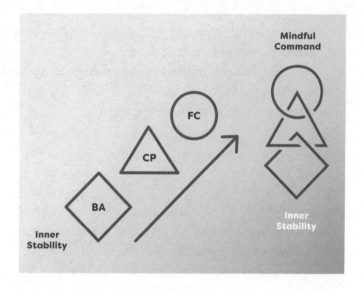

Your inner stability grows when you bring your clear intention and calm attention consistently to life. It's a practice that becomes a way of being, bringing a feeling of safety and constancy to the uncertainty, volatility and chaos of life. Your inner stability equips you to hold the space for others to access theirs. Over time, your stable inner leader becomes who you are.

Growing your capacity to feel stable inside is like drip-feeding water into a large wobbly bowl. As the bowl fills up with water it becomes more stable. Too much water at once and the bowl topples over; not enough and the bowl continues to wobble. When the bowl is full of water, it's stable and still. And when you look into the clear, calm water held by the bowl, you see yourself reflected there.

There are many ways to drip-feed your inner stability. They include the food and drink you consume; the quality of your sleep; how you breathe and exercise; quiet time in nature; and connecting to the important moments of life. These basic forms of self-care are as necessary as they are obvious.

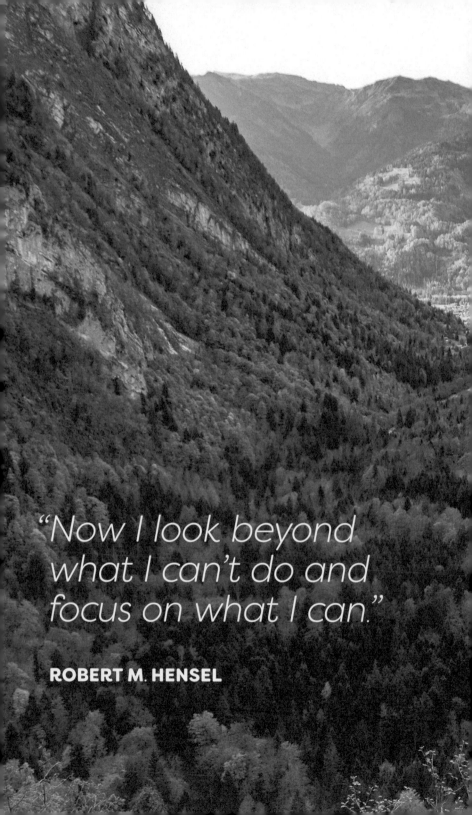

"Now I look beyond
what I can't do and
focus on what I can."

ROBERT M. HENSEL

INNER STABILITY DRIP-FEED (1):

MINDFUL WELLBEING

Living in the food capital of the world is a genuine delight. Every day at around midday in towns and cities all over France, shops close and restaurants fill up with people taking a two-hour lunch break to enjoy their food, perhaps some wine, and each other's company.

French food has a rich and colourful heritage of fresh produce and simple flavours, exquisitely prepared and presented to create a feast for the eyes. This last part is important because it engages all our senses, and the eating experience is more wholistically nourishing.

The vegetarian food on our Evolving Leadership retreats is prepared by my friend, collaborator and wonderful local chef, Jess de Jong. As important as her culinary skills are, the loving care with which she prepares every meal is also evident. "Food for the soul" is how many describe it; and they go home determined to change their eating habits – simply because of how her food has made them feel.

For some of the meals we engage in a practice called mindful eating. We do this together as a group in silence, bringing our clear intention and calm attention to what for most people is a novel practice. Everyone is invited to start by simply looking at the food on their plate and taking a moment to appreciate everything that went into putting it there, right from its origin. Then to savour each mouthful from the first to the last, chewing it slowly and tuning into the flavour and texture of the food. It can be so alien to people's experience of eating that it feels extremely uncomfortable. This is part of the practice.

Good food, lovingly prepared and eaten mindfully, is deeply nourishing. And so is good sleep. Allowing the brain and body to power down is vital to our wellbeing. At 10pm each evening, following a period of guided meditation, we invite the group to transition to 'quiet time.' Everyone – particularly busy working parents – appreciates the experience of their mind and body being allowed to rest and recuperate. And many take that habit home with them too.

Before breakfast the following day we meet for yoga practice with my friend, collaborator and yoga teacher, Julia Barnes. She works with the group to stretch and open the body, especially in the hips and shoulders. This allows the breath to flow and enables the body to move more freely and sit more comfortably on the ground.

The embodied practice of eating, drinking, breathing, exercising and sleeping mindfully brings greater physiological balance and harmony. You feel clearer, more stable and more like yourself.

INNER STABILITY DRIP-FEED (2):

SPENDING QUIET TIME IN NATURE

When I think of spending time in nature, I see a mountain, I see water and I see a willow tree.

The willow tree is rooted, but not rigid; stable, but not inflexible. Reaching up to the sky, and able to bend and twist. Working with the elements, rather than fighting them.

In the first year of our Evolving Leadership programme, the group spent a night in a mountain refuge (we usually do). It was early summer, and our guide – my friend, collaborator and mountain guide, Arno de Jong – drew our attention to the effects of the alpine winter weather on the surrounding landscape. In the middle of it all was a willow tree. Windswept, buffeted by the elements, the tree was slowly regaining its upright form after weeks of being buried beneath an avalanche.

Willow wood weighs light (whereas oak wood, for example, weighs heavier). It's also the wood that cricket bats are made of. It's light, and strong enough to be struck repeatedly by a solid, fast-moving cricket ball without splintering or denting. Willow has the strength of oak and the lightness of pine. Its roots reach deep for the water they need to survive. This deep rootedness supports its capacity to bend and flex, while remaining stable.

"We all need to be more like a willow tree," someone observed. Be More Willow became the group motto.

Standing among trees of any kind is a great place to practise grounding yourself. Next time you're walking in woodland, try this:

Pick a spot and stand there for a while.

Press the soles of your feet into the earth
and reach up to the sky. Take a long, slow,
deep breath.

Contemplate the qualities of the trees
surrounding you.

What do you learn about inner stability
from this?

Another way we explore inner stability with our evolving leaders is through Qigong. My friend, collaborator
and Chinese medical practitioner, Ben Cox, takes the
group out into nature and teaches them how to stand
and move in a way that feels rooted, stable and balanced.
For many, the slow, deceptively simple movements are
surprisingly challenging; not because they're techni-
cally difficult, but because the leaders in the group are
used to a more hurried pace. The deliberate, repetitive
nature of the movements can leave them feeling unsat-
isfied, with energy aching to be burned off.

Yes. Because inner stability invites us to Be More Willow.

There are few things in life I like better than hiking up a mountain. But sometimes it's enough simply to sit and look at one. Withstanding all weathers,

the mountain seems imperturbable. Majestic, yet grounded; solid, but not fixed; still, while moving and changing constantly.

When I'm struggling with something difficult, I sit and look at a mountain. I'm looking at the mountain, and the mountain is looking back at me. As I sit there, I tune into all my senses – noticing what I see, hear, smell, taste and touch. I look out at the mountain and up to the sky and allow myself to take it all in.

My mind is interested and effortlessly drawn into what *Inner Game* author Timothy Gallwey calls "natural focus": a relaxed, unforced concentration. No tension, no straining or squinting, no control. And no thinking hard.

I become aware of the physical sensations and the different muscles at work even as I sit. Feeling my body as it is, and not as I think it should be. My struggle melts away. I feel centred and stable. As if the mountain is showing me how to be.

If you live in flatter country, or on the coast, or in a city, and your landscape is different to mine, perhaps there's something you pass by every day that you could pause and simply look at? When you do, try this:

Right where you are, pick out a single small object – perhaps a single (wild) flower or a leaf or a twig. Feel it in your hands. Hold it to your face and smell it. Scrutinize it in tiny detail.

When you're ready, lift your gaze and look out. Soften your focus; take in the whole landscape before you.

Contract and expand your view.

Now open all your senses to the experience.

What do you learn about inner stability from this?

As a leader, parent, partner, friend, you may feel pulled and pushed in different directions and buffeted from one thing to the next. Every so often, your mind and body need to feel what it's like to be somewhere in the middle of it all. Centred. Still. OK with what is right there and open to what lies ahead.

Yes. Because inner stability invites us to Be More Mountain.

———————

With mountains come rivers, lakes, streams and waterfalls.

Standing close to this beauty – known as the Queen of the Alps – you see, hear and feel the power of the cascading water carving its centuries-old path through the limestone rock. It generates a roaring sound that carries for miles; and a strong, cooling breeze that causes nearby trees to bend and sway.

At the base of the waterfall are rock pools. They are calm and quiet – the same water in different form. Further on the water changes again into another thunderous cascade; and further on still into more pools of still water. And so, the water flows, weaving its way down the mountain and pouring eventually into the river below.

Next time you're out in nature and come across any kind of water – river, stream, waterfall, lake, pond, reservoir – or, indeed, if you're by the sea, try this:

Pick a spot and stand there for a while,
as still as you can, and simply look at
the water.

Notice how the water flows. Look for its
movement and its stillness. How are they
the same? How are they different?

What do you learn about inner stability
from this?

Observe any skilled sportsperson, dancer, gymnast, martial arts practitioner, or performer of any kind, and look for the moments of stillness in their movement.

Stillness is the base of movement. When there is both, there is flow.

Yes. Because inner stability invites us to Be More Waterfall: by finding the stillness within and moving from there.

INNER STABILITY DRIP-FEED (3):

CONNECTING TO THE IMPORTANT MOMENTS OF LIFE

Every morning before my husband and I sit down to breakfast, we light a candle – a sturdy, thick, pillar candle – and place it at the centre of the table.

"Shall we light the candle?" Simon asks.

"Yes," I reply.

And I stop what I'm doing to watch him take a match from its box, strike it and light the candle. We give this our full attention, in silence.

When breakfast is over, Simon asks:

"Shall we blow out the candle?"

"Yes," I reply.

He picks up the candle and steps out onto our balcony. Silhouetted by the mountain, he gently blows the candle out. I give my full attention to the sight, sound, smell, taste and feel of it all.

We could equally well light and extinguish the candle randomly while chatting. It would still be there, alight, in the middle of our table. But it would be a very different experience.

For us, this morning ritual is a moment to pause and be thankful. As I watch the flame rise and rest in its stable glow, I feel grateful to be alive. Later, when the flame disappears in a puff of smoke, I'm reminded that whatever arises that day will pass. As indeed, one day, will we.

Our clear intention and calm attention transform this simple event into something of greater significance. And with it comes a feeling of inner peace and stability: knowing that whatever happens we, individually and together, will be OK.

The more of ourselves Simon and I bring to this daily ritual, the more we gain from it. Our clear intention and calm attention nourish a feeling of inner stability, which in turn helps us feel clear and calm.

Without clarity and calm, stability is shaky. Without stability, clarity and calm are brittle.

———————————

Ritual has many different forms. Everyday rituals like greetings, meetings, weddings, birthdays, holidays, sports, births, funerals, or seasonal ceremonies and traditions are an opportunity to gather around something of common significance. What any of them means to the people involved depends on how they personally relate to it.

On 6th May 2023, in Westminster Abbey in London, Charles III was crowned King of the United Kingdom. This was ritual on a grand scale: 10,000 Armed Forces personnel, guests and spectators from multiple faiths, cultures and communities across the United Kingdom, numerous carriages, street parties, and a lot of pomp and sparkle. All for a man, as an *Economist* article put it, to be "given a hat."[11]

While some aspects of the traditional service were changed to reflect societal changes, the centuries-old Coronation Oath remained the same. Charles swore to govern the peoples according to their laws and customs, to act with justice and mercy, and to the utmost of his power preserve the doctrine and worship of the Church of England.

Not everyone could subscribe to that. People of other faiths, or no faith, could not relate to the coronation as the consecration of the monarch by the Christian God. Buddhist teacher and writer, Vishvapani, shared his alternative intention to keep in mind the central message of a book Charles had authored years before:[12] that seeing the harmony of things opens up a deeper connection to life.

"Sensing that life is inherently meaningful changes everything," Vishvapani observed. "It means that deep within us lie the seeds of wisdom, and engaging with them requires us to engage with a spiritual dimension to our existence. To restore balance in the world, we must restore balance in ourselves."

The Unitarians' Chief Officer, Liz Slade, suggested we might use the occasion to make an oath that felt more personally meaningful to us. She offered the following collective pledge as a starting point, and recommended we strengthen the idea and our commitment to it by making it part of a ritual – to give the words "more of a felt sense of occasion."

> I commit to use the utmost of my power to
> act with love for all people and all of nature,
> in my home, in my community, and for our
> whole society.

Committing to use the "utmost of our power" is an act of courage that requires us to connect with a deep sense of what matters most in our lives: in this case, love. Love for everyone and everything, everywhere. It's a practice for life, and ritual helps us embed it within us.

Liz suggested we might light a candle and then say the oath, or say it with a dandelion clock in our hands. When we've finished saying the words out loud, we might simply listen to the silence and then, when we're ready, blow the candle out or blow away the dandelion seeds.

What brings significance to this ritual is the quality of your intention and attention. In other words, what it means to you is up to you.

> Think of a moment of transition in your daily
> life which is important but has somehow
> lost its significance over time: like greeting
> your partner at the end of the working day;
> dropping your child/ren off at school; or
> calling your mother.
>
> What is one simple thing you could do
> in these routine moments to generate a
> greater sense of connection?

At the beginning and end of our five-day Evolving Leadership retreats, we invite the participants into a simple opening and closing ritual created by my friend, collaborator and ritual designer Viktor Smålänning.

The purpose of the ritual is to allow space for the group to transition from and to their everyday life into the retreat. It's an important moment, to which we invite the group to give their full attention. Their focused attention supports both their own inner stability and the collective stability of the group.

The opening ritual involves a river, a bridge, a muslin bag and our individual commitment to the process.

We walk together in silence from the retreat centre to the river nearby. This is a meditative walk, in which we individually explore what inner obstacles might prevent us from participating fully in the retreat: things like limiting beliefs, self-judgment, judgment of others, or mental and emotional commitments to be elsewhere. The invitation is not to permanently let go of these things, but to park them for the duration of our retreat.

For every inner obstacle we identify, we find a different object in nature – a twig, leaf, stone, flower, berry, etc. – to represent it. We place each object into the muslin bag, but first we hold it for a moment and intentionally 'infuse' it with the quality of the obstacle. For example, if a workplace challenge were an obstacle for you and you picked a stone to represent it, you would see the stone as holding that challenge for you for the period of the retreat.

We each find a place along the riverbank to hang our bag. Leaving the bag there signifies a choice to park our inner obstacles there too. We then come together again as a group next to the bridge. Having chosen what to leave outside the retreat, it's time to choose what to bring with us into it.

The bridge is the threshold between being in and out of the retreat. We invite everyone to cross it in a way that embodies how they commit to showing up. For example, if someone commits to being joyful, they might skip across the bridge with open arms. The idea is to let our body manifest our choice in whatever way feels right to us; and only if we want to. This is a personal commitment we each make with ourselves.

We have now formally stepped into the retreat. We're present and ready for the work ahead.

On the morning of the last day, we do the same thing in reverse. We cross the bridge in a way that embodies how we commit to showing up in our life. The retreat is now officially over.

Before leaving the river, we all go and find our bag. The invitation now is either to empty its contents into the river and watch them sink or float away; or keep them (some or all). Either is fine: what matters is the personal commitment that accompanies our choice.

Collective ritual has the power to speak to the deep human longing within us. It forges a sense of wholeness, and a reassuring sense of connection. We become part of a bigger story.

INNER STABILITY
IN PRACTICE

Peter was the executive director of a high-performing, thousand-seat call centre in a multinational company. Every morning at 08:30–08:45, whoever in the 14-person leadership team was there that day would meet in the call centre lobby for a stand-up check in. One minute per person to share key objectives for the day ahead, where they were planning to be that day, and anything they might need from the rest of the team. Everyone else was welcome to attend. This simple ritual took place every day, without fail.

Peter had been in the role for six years when he was informed of the board of directors' decision to close the call centre down. Everyone, including him – the 13 directors, 100 supervisors and 886 agents – were going to lose their jobs.

This was deeply destabilizing. Everything Peter and his people had worked hard to build was about to be pulled apart. While he had no choice but to accept there was no way out, he was determined to guide the right way through.

Peter did two important things: he personally engaged in securing follow-on employment for his people; and he invested in creating the right conditions for them to focus primarily on what they had gained from the past few years, and not on what they were about to lose. He knew that staying connected to the purpose and value of their work would give them something solid to believe in during the tough months ahead.

In doing this for his people, Peter was standing calmly for what mattered most.

In the week that the call centre was due to close, Peter took the entire leadership team to the beach. He spread out a large blanket and invited them all to sit. Then he gave them each a tiny glass jar with a lid. One by one, they shared what they were grateful for from their experience of working together. When they'd said what they wanted to say, they filled their jar with sand and took it home.

My friend and collaborator, Christina Kisley, was with them that day. She'd been their coach for most of the time Peter had been in the role. She still has her jar of sand, as does Peter and his team. That was 14 years ago. The jar, the sand and what they represent mean as much to them now as they did then.

———————

Julie was juggling her responsibilities as global head of research and development for a large multinational company with parenting a young family and overseeing the construction of their new home.

She liked to feel efficient. Efficiency, she said, was her key to feeling peaceful and calm.

"I'm not feeling as peaceful and calm as I'd like to," she told me.

I asked Julie if she could remember a recent moment when she had felt peaceful and calm. She could. It was a surprise family picnic her partner had organized for her birthday a few weeks before. It was in the country, at a spot near a lake, and they had all gone swimming.

"What was efficient about it?" I asked.

"Nothing," she said, smiling. "If anything, it was slightly chaotic, and not how I would have planned it. But it was so nice just to be there."

So nice just to be there. What was nice about it? How did she feel? Did she sense anything anywhere in her body?

Julie was able to describe the whole experience in quite some detail. When she had finished, I asked her how she felt now.

"Peaceful and calm."

"As peaceful and calm as you'd like to?"

"Yes. But this is easy. What's hard is feeling like this in real life."

Indeed. We all wrestle with this. We associate peace and calm with certain external conditions. And yes, when we're in nature, or with people we love, or doing things we enjoy, it's far easier to feel grounded, stable, peaceful, calm. The rest of life becomes something we have to get through to get there.

If you ever hear yourself saying, "I'll be happy when...," or "I'll be glad when this is over...," try asking yourself: "What part of me is in the way of being happy now?"

In the way of her feeling peaceful and calm was Julie's idea that this was only possible when everything was done well, successfully and without waste. And now, as she started to let that idea go, she was effectively changing her mind.

A change of mind changes everything.

Julie decided to take a long hard look at everything she was juggling, and which balls she could afford to drop, delegate or resource differently. She decided to start each day with a few minutes for herself: to simply sit, breathe, and do nothing other than sense and feel the peace and calm already there. And she took stock of the other ways she could drip feed her inner stability little by little every day. She picked a few and committed to doing them.

"I'm feeling a lot better," she told me later. "Not as peaceful and calm as I'd like to be but improving day to day."

She was on her way.

———————

The way is more important than the destination. For the purposes of inner stability, better to forget the destination and focus on the way.

As a leader, parent, partner, friend, the most important and the hardest of all our roles is being how we want to be now. "To be the change..." as Mahatma Gandhi is credited to have said. Here's the fuller version:

> We but mirror the world. All the tendencies present in the outer world are to be found in the world of our body. If we could change ourselves, the tendencies in the world would also change. As a man changes his own nature, so does the attitude of the world change toward him. This is the divine mystery supreme. A wonderful thing it is and the source of our happiness. We need not wait to see what others do.

No, we need not wait. The capacity to show up as your grounded, centred self, standing calmly for what matters, is something you can start building now.

FINDING YOUR OWN WAY

If you truly want to change how you show up in the world, you can.

You can let go of the ideas that limit you, and you can gently release the fears that stand in your way. You can open your mind to seeing things as they really are, to clarifying what matters most and to cultivating the courage to calmly do the right thing for the people you lead and love.

For this to happen, your cognitive understanding of what is needed is not enough. You have to embody what you've learned in a physical way. To show up with Mindful Command, you need to engage with the tools and practices that support it.

Any or all of them will help you on your way. Adapt and integrate them into your life and work in a way that works for you. Make them yours.

———————

Are you ready to find your way?

If you're wondering where to start, I recommend you first do the Mindful Command self-assessment starting on page 24 (or again if you did it earlier), and see what that tells you.

The gateway to any behavioural change is learning how to pause and create the space for the change to occur. Pausing to think, even for a few seconds, is a vital leadership skill in any situation. So, learning the pause tool on page 67 should be your next step.

Then, having identified the situations that you find most challenging, experiment with the other tools and practices offered throughout the book. For example, the Balanced Awareness Pyramid, the Very Clear Ideas process, the Fearless Compassion reflective practices or any of the ways to drip-feed Inner Stability.

I've shared with you what has helped me. Please share with others whatever helps you. And let me know how you get on. Then we can all learn from each other.

And if you need or want any support along your way, please get in touch (contact details below). I work with leaders one-to-one, in teams and on our annual Evolving Leadership programme.

———————

I wish you all the best for your journey ahead, wherever it may take you.

With love from the mountain.

Sally-Anne

Samoëns, Haute-Savoie
August 2023

skilfulleaders.com
sally-anne@skilfulleaders.com

NOTES

1. See Chapter Five.

2. Documented from crew accounts in *Undersea Warriors* by Iain Ballantyne (Pegasus Books, 2019).

3. In those days, Post Traumatic Stress Syndrome was not recognized, and no help had been available to them.

4. https://thehappystartupschool.com

5. More on this in Chapter 4.

6. If you find a guided practice helpful, tune into my short video series 21 Days on the Mountain, freely available on my SkilfulLeaders YouTube channel.

7. Vipassana means to see things as they really are and is one of India's most ancient meditation techniques.

8. DSL did not close but it did eventually relocate to a site where its upkeep could be assured.

9. Following the Iran–Iraq war and the subsequent attacks on shipping.

10. Governed by United Nations Security Council resolution 660.

11. The Economist, 6 May 2023. *Britain crowns Charles III its new king.* Available at: https://www.economist.com/ britain/2023/05/04/britain-crowns-charles-iii-its-new-king.

12. *Harmony: A New Way of Looking at Our World*, 2010.

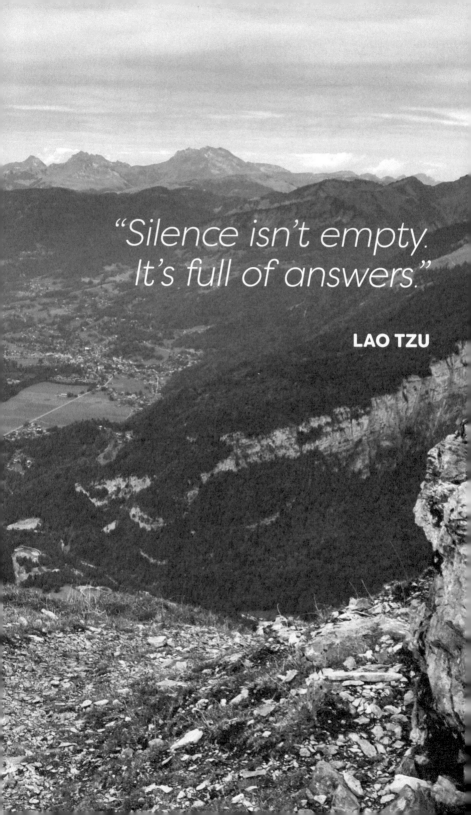

"Silence isn't empty.
It's full of answers."

LAO TZU

ACKNOWLEDGMENTS

I owe this book to all the leaders and teachers I've worked with, all the teams I've led, and to all the mistakes I've made.

I am especially grateful to my husband Simon Airey, my friend and collaborator Christina Kisley, and my editor Clare Christian, for their patient reading and rereading of the book draft and their brilliant feedback.

I also deeply value the wise contributions of Charles Davies, Max St John, Ben Cox, Stephen Burt and Viktor Lysell Smålänning to the work that this book describes.

For the graphic artwork, my thanks to the multi-talented Polina Brodowski. And for the photography, thank you Simon Airey.